# GHOST
# NOTES

To Jed,

Greetings from the

Note Taker —

'01

Cheers

*[signature]*

# GHOST NOTES

## Haunted Happenings on California's Historic Monterey Peninsula

As recorded by
**Randall A. Reinstedt**

**Ghost Town Publications**
Carmel, California

If bookstores in your area do not carry *Ghost Notes,* copies may be obtained by writing to . . .

## GHOST TOWN PUBLICATIONS

P.O. Drawer 5998
Carmel, CA 93921

Other books by Randall A. Reinstedt, offered by Ghost Town Publications, are:

GHOSTS, BANDITS AND LEGENDS of Old Monterey
MONTEREY'S MOTHER LODE
SHIPWRECKS AND SEA MONSTERS of California's Central Coast
TALES, TREASURES AND PIRATES of Old Monterey
GHOSTLY TALES AND MYSTERIOUS HAPPENINGS of Old Monterey
WHERE HAVE ALL THE SARDINES GONE?
MYSTERIOUS SEA MONSTERS of California's Central Coast
INCREDIBLE GHOSTS of Old Monterey's HOTEL DEL MONTE
INCREDIBLE GHOSTS of the BIG SUR COAST

10 9 8 7 6 5 4 3

Manufactured in the United States of America

Library of Congress Catalog Number: 88-082533
ISBN 0-933818-09-2

Edited by John Bergez
Book design by John Edeen
Cover design by Ed Greco

*This book is dedicated to those
who shared with me their tales
of the strange and unexplained*

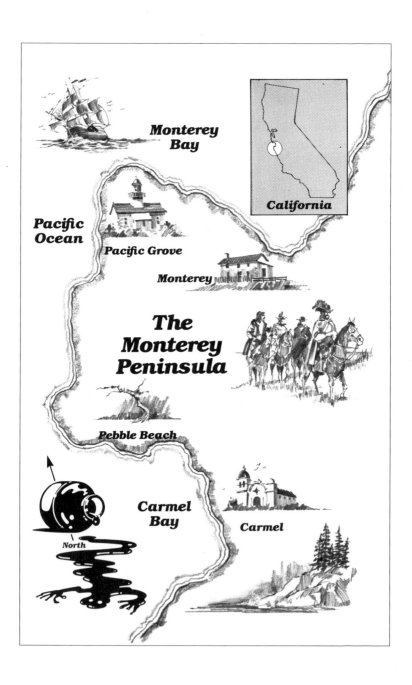

Monterey Bay

California

Pacific Ocean

Pacific Grove

Monterey

The
Monterey
Peninsula

Pebble Beach

North

Carmel Bay

Carmel

# Contents

# Introduction

I didn't start out to be a ghost hunter.

In fact, it would be truer to say that the many ghosts that seem to populate the beautiful and historic Monterey Peninsula came hunting for me—as they do for anyone who is inquisitive about the area's rich and colorful past. If you are receptive to the subject of ghostly happenings, you'll find them lurking everywhere you look, from Monterey's aged adobes to Pacific Grove's charming Victorians, from quaint cottages in Carmel to secluded mansions in Pebble Beach.

So many are the stories, in fact, that even after several publications on this subject, my files are bulging with notes of ghostly happenings in and around the Monterey Peninsula, most of them never before published. It is these "ghost notes"—collected over a twenty-year period—which I now present in book form, in approximately the order in which I first recorded them. I hope they will be of interest to residents and visitors who wish to know more about the history and lore of our scenic area as well as to readers with a special interest in tales of the supernatural.

In looking at the Golden State's central coast, one must admit that—if there is a community that *should* boast an abundance of ghostly tales—Monterey would have to be considered a likely candidate. Founded in 1770, Monterey served as California's capital under both Spanish and Mexican rule, and is among the most historic towns in the western United States. More importantly for ghost enthusiasts,

1

it boasts many of its original buildings, with a surprising number of them dating back to the mid-1800s (including the famed Robert Louis Stevenson House). A number of the tales reported in this book concern these aged structures, many of which can be visited by the public. Colorful Cannery Row and the United States Naval Postgraduate School (site of Monterey's old Hotel Del Monte) are among the other local sites whose claims to ghostly fame are as impressive as their other historic credentials. I hope that readers of this book will enjoy learning some of the history of these sites and structures along with the eerie tales associated with them.

## A journey of discovery . . .

These notes represent a journey of discovery for me that began, appropriately enough, in 1970, Monterey's bicentennial year. It was then that my first account of ghostly happenings appeared in print. By that time I had been collecting information about my native area for several years, but it was only after this article was published that my real interest began in tales of the strange and unexplained.

Entitled "Ghosts of Old Monterey," the article, which appeared as a two-part series in a local magazine, generated considerable interest in the subject of the supernatural in and around California's scenic central coast. It also prompted several individuals to contact me and to share their experiences. I soon learned that the fear of being ridiculed prohibited some people from discussing experiences they considered odd, or out of the ordinary, with friends or family members. Instead, these individuals sought someone to talk to who expressed interest and who wouldn't think them peculiar. Accounts from such people, as well as from the numerous old-timers I had tracked down, prompted me to look at the subject of the supernatural with a more open mind and to begin recording many of the stories I heard.

2

At the start, I had no notion of eventually collecting these stories in book form. As a result, many of the accounts I recorded during my initial years of "ghost note" taking were not as detailed as they could or should have been. However, as the accounts grew in number and detail, and as additional tales came to light in the course of other history-oriented research, they began to take on the look of a small book. This book became a reality in 1971. Originally published as *Ghosts of Old Monterey*, the book has gone through several subsequent printings and today is known as *Ghosts, Bandits and Legends of Old Monterey*. Currently available in selected Monterey Bay area bookstores and gift shops, the publication continues to be popular among visitors and residents.

With this as the beginning, my ghost note file continued to expand through additional contacts, research, and interviews of old-timers. Eventually this material made a second ghost book irresistible. Published in 1977, *Ghostly Tales and Mysterious Happenings of Old Monterey* touched on various areas of Monterey County in addition to the Monterey Peninsula, including the beautiful San Antonio Valley and its historic mission.

One might think that with two books on *local* ghosts I would be content to forget about the subject of the supernatural and concentrate on other aspects of Monterey history. This, however, was not to be, for the stories continued to accumulate. As it happened, many of them were associated with Monterey's fabulous Hotel Del Monte (as noted earlier, now the United States Naval Postgraduate School). In its day, the Del Monte was an internationally known resort (described as "The Most Elegant Seaside Establishment in the World"). As its centennial year (1980) drew near, few people seemed to be aware of the occasion, despite the hotel's significant place in Monterey history. As I considered the multitude of ghost stories that were connected with the hotel and its buildings, I decided to celebrate its centennial with a short book about them. Published in June, 1980—one hundred years to the month after the spacious spa first opened—*Incredible Ghosts of Old Monterey's Hotel Del Monte* proved to be the start of my "Incredible Ghosts" series.*

The second book in the "Incredible Ghosts" series was published in 1981 and is called *Incredible Ghosts of the Big Sur Coast*. While it includes several "traditional" ghost stories, the book also documents a number of historical happenings (such as the dramatic wreck of the dirigible *Macon*) and interesting accounts of the strange and unexplained.

Since the Big Sur book was published, I have been involved in several other writing projects. During this period my ghost note file continued to expand as more people shared their stories with me. It was while I was working on my fifth children's book, *The Strange Case of the Ghosts of the Robert Louis Stevenson House*, that the idea for *Ghost Notes* began to take shape. As I was checking the various Robert Louis Stevenson House accounts I had previously recorded, I began to appreciate the quantity of ghost-related material I had collected over the years—material that seemed too compelling to be left in unread files. Gradually I began to think about collecting these unvarnished tales into a book of "ghost notes." The work you are reading is the result.

## About this book . . .

As you will see, after some early undated tales, this work consists of accounts I recorded from various sources, arranged according to the date when I first learned of them.

---

* Like most of my publications, this book not only tells about the structure's strange happenings, but also includes a brief history of the hotel and how it came to be. For those who may be interested in learning more about this "Queen of American Watering Places," the first half of the book discusses the history of the grand resort (including its fabulous Seventeen Mile Drive and its numerous California "firsts"), while the second half tells about many of the ghostly happenings that have taken place there.

While some of the notes present full and detailed descriptions of odd occurrences, others are jottings that only tease us into wanting to know more. I believe that even these "teasers" are worth sharing, both because they will allow others to share my personal journey of discovery and because—taken together—all the tales, hints, and anecdotes do suggest that the unexplained (and perhaps unexplainable) is far more common than most people imagine.

Although I have elaborated on the notes in preparing them for publication, I have tried to retain the flavor of jottings that originally were written in journal form, at a time when I had no thoughts of putting them together in a book. I hope that in this way readers can share the experience of suddenly coming across a new tale—or additional information about (or confirmation of) a story recorded previously (sometimes years earlier). Details such as where I was at the time, or how I came to meet the person who shared a story with me, illustrate that one never knows when or where a promising story, a historical anecdote, or an intriguing tale of the strange and unexplained will suddenly surface.

Readers will note that in most cases I have omitted the names of my informants, as well as of the individuals included in their accounts, in order to safeguard their privacy. For similar reasons I have generally omitted the addresses of the buildings where ghostly events are said to have occurred, with the exception of a number of state- and city-owned structures that may be viewed or visited by the public (often brief historical sketches are provided for these structures).

As was previously hinted at, the accounts tend to become more elaborate as the book goes on. This is largely due to the time and effort I put into documenting stories of the supernatural as my interest in the subject grew. Of course, the amount of information I was able to record depended on how much the person I was talking to was able—or willing—to share. In the case of accounts taken from diaries, letters, newspapers, and other written sources, I was often limited to the information they contained.

Because of the date sequence in which the tales are recorded, it is difficult to read all the accounts about one building or site in consecutive order. For this reason, an Index of Locations is included at the end of the book listing both the text mentions of well-known buildings and the illustrations contained in this work.

As you read these accounts, please remember that I cannot vouch for the authenticity of each tale, as I was not the person who experienced the events reported here. In almost every case, my part has been to record the incidents as they were recounted to me, often by the person who experienced the happening. This I have done to the best of my ability, and along the way I hope that I have helped to preserve a little of the lore of old Monterey and its neighboring communities. I also hope I have helped each reader realize that history is not cut and dried. As a matter of fact, certain aspects of our history may continue to take place before our very eyes!

Randall A. Reinstedt

# Setting the Scene

Although most of the ghost notes found within this work are recorded in the date order I learned of them, I must admit that I can't be sure when I first became aware of the following incident from the earliest days of Spanish California. Over the years I read about it (or accounts similar to it) in more than one source. In reviewing my notes and preparing them for publication, I became convinced that this episode was a fitting way to begin this book, since it takes us back to the beginning of Monterey's recorded history. More importantly, it helps set the scene for the many mysterious happenings that have taken place in the area since then . . .

## The cross seemed to reach to the heavens . . .

To appreciate this tale we must look at Alta (Upper) California of 1769. It was in this year that Gaspar de Portola, Governor of Baja (Lower) California, set out from San Diego on a land search for the bay of Monterey. (Monterey Bay had gained its name from the Basque merchant-navigator Sebastian Vizcaino in 1602.) Not recognizing the bay when he came upon it—as the wind-blown waters didn't resemble the safe and secure harbor Vizcaino had described—Portola continued his trek north and discovered San Francisco Bay and California's majestic redwood trees in the process. With the discovery of San Francisco's vast natural harbor, Portola realized he had gone too far and returned to the wind-swept waters of Monterey Bay. Upon rounding the inlet the Portola party made camp on the southerly shores of the Monterey Peninsula (near the present-day Carmel Mission). While resting on the banks of Carmel Bay, Portola and his men spent several days scouting the area and preparing for their march back to San Diego.

Still not recognizing Monterey Bay—even though their camp was but a short distance from it—the Portola party erected a cross on its shore and on the shore of neighboring Carmel Bay, complete with messages to seafarers telling of their lack of success. They then began their long journey south.

After many hardships the exhausted men reached San Diego Bay. Here Portola discussed the expedition with Father Junipero Serra, the founder and leader of California's famed mission chain. Upon checking the facts, and reviewing the Vizcaino chronicle, they decided that Portola had indeed found Monterey Bay but had failed to recognize it because of Vizcaino's overly enthusiastic description.

A second expedition was soon decided upon, and plans were again made to seek Monterey Bay. However, this time the men were to go by both land and sea. After a much-needed rest, Portola again began the trek north, with Serra to follow aboard the Spanish supply ship *San Antonio.*

When the Spanish reached the elusive bay on this second expedition, the water was calm, and it resembled the bay Vizcaino had described. Portola and Serra soon rendezvoused on the shore, where mass was said and an accompanying ceremony was performed in the shade of a nearby oak tree. (It was under this same tree that mass had been said by Father Antonio de la Ascension of the Vizcaino expedition in 1602.) Among the events that took place during this June 3, 1770, ceremony was the founding of Serra's second Alta California mission. Also of importance was the founding of the Presidio of Monterey and of Monterey as a community. With the establishment of this bayside town, Alta California gained a capital, and the colorful history of this north coast outpost began.

Fittingly enough, these events also marked the beginning of the many mysterious happenings that have become such an interesting part of this history-rich area. When the Portola party reached Monterey Bay on their second expedition, they found the cross they had erected on their first visit, still in place. However, accompanying the cross were a variety of objects, including arrows placed around the cross and pointing to it, a cluster of feathers (thought to have been from an eagle), a string of fresh fish (perhaps sardines), and a neat mound of mussels.

The Spanish were mystified as to the significance of these decorations. It wasn't until sometime later that Indians of the area told the padres that during the night the cross had become bright—almost as if it were lit up—and had appeared to reach far up into the heavens! Awed by this magical (or, perhaps I should say, mystical) experience, the Indians had brought peace offerings to the visitors' god.

With this account of a strange and unexplained happening having taken place in the Monterey area over two centuries ago, the stage is set for more of the same. So snuggle up before a crackling fire, and read these notes—out loud, if you please, in your best whispery voice . . . so the unseen things lurking nearby can enjoy these ghostly tales right along with you.

# In the Beginning
## (1970–1976)

As explained in the Introduction, it was only gradually that I became aware of, and fascinated by, the many strange stories associated with the Monterey area. At first I was not scrupulous about recording such things as the date when I first learned of a particular incident, so the ghost notes in this section are undated.

Many of the accounts I learned about early on have been incorporated into my previous ghost books. With a few exceptions, they are omitted from this collection, which concentrates on notes that were taken after my fourth ghost book was published in August, 1981. Almost all the tales you are about to read are being published for the first time.

A couple of previously recorded incidents, however, are of special interest—especially in light of stories that will be reported in subsequent notes—and so are related here in some detail.* Coincidentally, I first learned about both of these events during Monterey's bicentennial year of 1970. As you will discover, both concern sites that will come up repeatedly in the "supernatural" history of Monterey . . .

---

* Both are treated briefly in my book *Ghosts, Bandits and Legends of Old Monterey.*

# The dog was soon locked in combat . . .

In June of 1970, while seeking ghostly tales for a magazine article, I visited Monterey's Royal Presidio Chapel and its old rectory. The Royal Presidio Chapel is also known as San Carlos Cathedral, and today is Monterey's main Catholic church. It seems fitting that these notes begin in this section of old Monterey, as the chapel is one of California's most historic structures. However, even though this landmark dates back to the late 1700s and boasts its own collection of strange tales, it is its old rectory next door that the majority of the stories are about. Incidentally, certain sources indicate that the old rectory was built atop an earlier rectory building, which was destroyed by fire. If this information is accurate, one can't help but wonder whether—in some way—it helps to explain the many ghostly happenings reported here.

My quest for information turned up a wealth of accounts: the sound of rocking chairs rocking (where no chairs existed) . . . the discovery of a "mystery room" that hadn't been used for years . . . strange and unexplained shadows in the windows . . . the sighting of a dead priest who had lived in the building for many years . . . candles that moved of their own accord . . . books that fell from shelves and opened to places where money had been hidden . . . not to mention the more common ghostly occurrences of doors opening and closing, lights blinking off, and strange noises being heard. These reports were related by a number of reliable sources, including individuals connected with the church, a former local policeman, and the owner of a Peninsula-based security firm.

Clearly, the old rectory abounds in strange tales. Here is one that was touched on in my original ghost book and has since become a Peninsula favorite.

As the story begins, late one night a security patrol officer pulled to a stop in front of the Royal Presidio Chapel and its neighboring old rectory. Upon getting out of the car, the officer and his German shepherd attack dog started up the walkway toward the rectory. As they neared the main entrance, the dog suddenly became spooked and refused to go any further. Shining his flashlight on the shepherd, the officer was surprised to see it cowering and trying to slink away. Concerned as to what was happening—especially since the dog had never before shown any sign of fear—the officer yanked on the choke chain and commanded the shepherd to "Come!" Acting as if it didn't hear the command, or feel the tug of the chain, the dog continued to whimper and whine and try to get away.

It was obvious that the animal sensed something he didn't, so the officer decided to seek company as he checked the building. Returning to the front sidewalk, the officer and his dog headed for the new rectory on the opposite side of the church, where they were greeted by a priest. Upon hearing the story, the priest agreed to accompany them to see whether he could help determine what had disturbed the dog.

As they approached the old rectory, the shepherd reacted as it had before, making it clear it wanted nothing to do with the building! Nevertheless, after considerable coaxing, pushing, and prodding, the men were able to get the dog inside.

Upon closing the door and flashing their lights around the hall, the men focused their beams on the dog to see how it reacted to being inside. To their amazement, instead of frantically clawing at the door in an effort to get out, the shepherd stood like a statue and stared at the darkened hallway. With its hair bristling, its eyes wide, its ears erect, and its nose quivering, the gallant animal suddenly growled and took a mighty leap into the darkness!

Almost yanking the choke chain out of the officer's hand, the shepherd apparently found its foe, for it was soon locked in combat with an unseen thing. The men watched in awe as the dog fought the invisible force. At one point the shepherd fell—or was thrown—to the floor, as something attacked it about the neck! But almost as quickly it escaped the grasp of whatever was attacking it and began to get the upper hand. At this time all four of its paws were off the floor as it apparently stood atop its foe and continued to fight!

Judging from the dog's behavior, its opponent had soon had enough and after escaping from the shepherd's grasp it headed for a nearby flight of stairs. Trying to give chase, the shepherd succeeded in pulling the choke chain from the officer's hand, only to lose its adversary on the staircase. Standing on the steps and glancing back at the men (who had followed its pursuit with the beams of their flashlights), the dog seemed to have a bewildered look on its face, as if to ask, "What was it? Where did it go?" Of course, the priest and the police officer were just as baffled!

When I first recorded this tale, I talked to both of the men who were involved. The interviews were conducted separately, and each individual told me the same story in different words. Since then, one of the men has died (as has the dog), and the other man has left the area. In looking back, I can only say that of the hundreds of tales I have heard regarding the strange and unexplained, I would have to place this one near the top if I were asked to list the events I have recorded that I consider the most believable, and that I put the most faith in.

## The Lady in Black . . .

The second "special interest" event I wish to relate took place at Monterey's historic Robert Louis Stevenson House. Discussed in various publications (including the *New York Times*), the story is one of the best-known ghost stories on the California coast.

Monterey's Robert Louis Stevenson House, where the Scottish-born writer briefly lived in 1879, is located at 530 Houston Street. Today the building is owned by the state and contains one of the world's largest collections of Stevenson family pieces. Authentically restored and open to the public for guided tours, the building is a must for Stevenson enthusiasts.

And for ghost enthusiasts as well! Among the many ghostly happenings attributed to this structure are the mysterious movements of items in various rooms, a rocking chair in the Stevenson bedroom that rocks when no one is in it, door latches that rattle in the dead of night, the sounds of a woman singing when the house is locked and void of visitors, a "cheery" yellow rose that appeared in a locked upstairs room, and a manuscript left in a locked room that was edited by unseen hands.

Several of these incidents are described in my *Ghosts, Bandits and Legends* book, and a number of additional Stevenson House accounts will be found in this text. However, of all the building's many ghostly tales, the following famous incident deserves special mention. The event occurred late one afternoon as the Stevenson House guide was checking the structure prior to locking up for the night. As she walked down the upstairs hall, glancing into each room as she went, she was lost in thought and somewhat unconsciously going through the motions.

Upon nearing the end of the hall, the guide peered through the steel bars at the entrance to the children's nursery. (Full-length bars had been placed at the openings of some of the upstairs rooms to prevent visitors from disturbing the objects inside.) As the guide looked in the room, she saw a lady dressed in black standing at the foot of the bed. Costumed in clothes of long ago, the lady was gazing intently at the bed. Caught up in her own thoughts, the guide absent-mindedly mentioned that it was time to close and that the lady would have to leave.

Upon hearing her comment the "lady in black" turned, nodded, and smiled. With this acknowledgment the guide started toward the sunroom on the opposite side of the hall. Before she had taken more than a step or two, it suddenly dawned on her that nobody could have been in the nursery—

15

*especially anyone wearing the cumbersome clothing of the lady in black!* Spinning around and looking back into the nursery, the guide was shocked to discover that the lady had disappeared!

After the initial shock wore off, the guide reflected upon this strange sighting and wondered whether she might have seen the ghost of Mrs. Juan Girardin, the woman who owned the building when Robert Louis Stevenson stayed there in 1879. That year apparently was a very trying one for Mrs. Girardin. Not only did her husband die, but two of her grandchildren are said to have become gravely ill as the result of a fever epidemic that spread through Monterey County. Legend states that Mrs. Girardin spent countless hours in the nursery, nursing her grandchildren back to health. Thoughts such as these prompted the guide to wonder whether the ghost of Mrs. Girardin had perhaps returned to the building to be with her grandchildren in their time of need.

In concluding this note, I should mention that I have been unable to find any evidence of a life-threatening fever epidemic in Monterey County in 1879 (although one did spread through the area nine years before). Also, there is no proof that the room in which the lady in black appeared was a children's nursery in 1879—or any proof that it wasn't. However, there is no doubt that the guide's sighting of the lady in black—whoever she may be—is one of the Monterey area's most cherished ghost stories.

## A long-dead priest . . .

Having related in some detail two of Monterey's most popular ghost stories, I will proceed now with the unpublished ghost notes I have collected over the past twenty years. The following Carmel Mission account was recorded in the early 1970s. Although this church is symbolic of the early years of Spanish Monterey, the ghost in this tale is of far more recent vintage . . .

In talking to one of the Monterey Peninsula's best-known historians (now deceased), I was surprised to learn of a ghostly sighting he had made. My surprise stemmed from his no-nonsense approach to the subject of the supernatural. This attitude, combined with his international reputation as a historian, prompted me to put a great deal of faith in his account.

The two of us were sitting on a Carmel Mission bench, talking about history and interesting happenings of the past, when he mentioned the sighting. According to his story, one day when he was in the mission's beautiful front court he saw a man whose appearance perfectly matched that of a one-time friend, a long-dead Monterey priest. Amazed and alarmed by the uncanny likeness, he proceeded to follow the man. Upon catching up with him as they neared the church, the historian got an even greater shock. When he looked into the visiting priest's face, there was no doubt that he was the manifestation of his dead friend!*

## He drew his blade . . .

A local woman who has spent several years studying Monterey's adobes, and the people who lived in them, has turned up a tale about an Indian woman who died at or near the Robert Louis Stevenson House. Perhaps her account will offer Stevenson House buffs a clue to the many mysteries that surround this historic structure.

According to the story, one day long ago (thought to have been in the early 1900s) the Indian woman got into a violent argument with a saddle maker who lived in the

---

*While this account is short and somewhat lacking in detail, similar stories were related to me on two subsequent occasions by respected Monterey residents who knew the historian well. Both men felt the historian was serious about the sighting and that he was not the type of man to falsely report such an event. See "Brief and to the point," page 42, and "The ghostly image walked through the wall," page 73.

building. The heated exchange took place in the rear garden area or on the back balcony steps. As the argument escalated, the woman pulled a knife. Seeing her weapon, the saddle maker also reached for his blade, and in the fight that followed the woman was killed. If an incident such as this really did take place, one can't help but wonder if the ghostly guests that have been observed in and around the Stevenson House are in some way related to this tragic event.

## The night the light died . . .

Although this incident is not ghostly, it belongs in any collection of interesting anecdotes about old Monterey. Many years ago, long before the construction of Monterey's breakwater and the Municipal Wharf Number Two, Mary Little lived in a two-story structure in the area known as New Monterey. Because of her concern for the safety of seafarers who attempted to bring their vessels into the Monterey harbor at night, she kept a warning light burning in one of her upstairs windows. However, the night Mary died the lamp was not lit—and that very night a schooner was wrecked on the shore.

## The fisherman and his pine box were soon parted . . .

This story is adapted from an American Guide Series publication called the *Monterey Peninsula* (a WPA project written in 1946). Like the preceding account, it is not a ghostly tale, but it does befit the subject matter of these notes.

The original source does not indicate a date, but from the description it seems this tragicomic event probably took place prior to the turn of the century. Monterey is the scene, and the main player in this drama is a Portuguese fisherman who had recently died. Unfortunately for the fisherman—and perhaps even more so for his bereaved family and friends—the funeral procession took place soon after a heavy rain. Upon reaching the street leading to the cemetery, the driver of the wagon that carried the casket was forced to stop because of flooding in the street. Despite his misgivings, the women walking behind the wagon insisted that he go on, explaining that the body should not be halted on its way to heaven. Not wishing to argue, the driver slowly made his way into the water. The wagon sank deeper and deeper the further he went, and before long the only part of the wagon that was visible was the seat the driver was perched on. As he sat high and dry, with water swirling about him, the horse suddenly stopped. Not wanting to force the animal, which was obviously terrified, the driver proceeded to cut himself a plug of tobacco and wait. Concerned at the delay, the wailing mourners pleaded with the driver to continue, informing him it would not be good for the fisherman "to start his journey heavenward all wet." Finally the driver agreed to try and spur the horse on. Gingerly he touched him with his whip. Unfortunately, the already frightened animal overreacted to the whip and bolted forward. This sudden movement, combined with the swirling water, caused the coffin to slip out of the wagon. To make matters worse, the coffin lid had not been nailed shut, and with the coffin caught up in the swiftly flowing water, the fisherman and his pine box were soon parted! Followed by screaming mourners who ran beside the raging water, the body was washed down the street and into Monterey Bay!

With the whole town caught up in this tragic event, boats were soon searching the bay. Eventually, the body was found near the bay's southerly entrance and brought home. The next day the mourners tried again. This time, however, many Monterey residents joined the march behind the wagon, hoping to ensure that the fisherman's second trip to the cemetery was a safe one.

## The spirit moved on . . .

A few miles from Monterey is the small town of Castroville, known as the Artichoke Capital of the World. Among the stories connected with this community is a tale that tells of a ghostly presence, and of feelings of not being alone, that are associated with one of the community's dwellings. According to the occupants of a then-new house, the ghostly presence that frequented the premises made itself known in a number of ways—including not only noises, but an image revealed in the building's mirrors. After taking all they could of these manifestations, the occupants of the house decided to have the structure exorcised. Happily for them, the exorcism did seem to drive the presence from the building—but unhappily for the people living next door, it moved in with them!*

## Her automobile kept stalling . . .

While I'm still sorting through my early, unpublished notes, here is another mention of the Castroville area. As described in an August 1972 issue of the *Monterey Peninsula Herald*, a woman from Carmel experienced several frustrating delays as she attempted to drive through the crossroads at the intersection of Molera Road and Highway One. (The current Molera Road overpass had not yet been constructed.) Even though she drove a new and dependable car, she reported that over a period of nine months her

---

* Frustrated by this turn of events, the people who experienced the original incidents began checking into the area in which their house had been built, hoping to find a clue to the strange happenings. It was then they learned that long before their house was constructed, another dwelling had occupied the site. Unfortunately, my source didn't know whether their research revealed any odd or tragic incidents that had taken place in the original building—incidents that may have prompted a spirit to linger at the site.

automobile stalled eight times at this particular junction. A carburetor change and several other adjustments made little difference, as the car continued to stall. Completely frustrated and at a loss to explain the problem, she checked with several nearby garages and gas stations—only to learn that other motorists had reported similar problems at the same intersection!

## A terrible dream . . .

Between one and one-thirty in the morning a young Monterey man left the community of Watsonville (around the bay from Monterey) and headed for his Peninsula home at a high rate of speed. Having driven the road countless times, and already drowsy when he set out, he was in something of a sleep stupor as he bypassed the community of Castroville. Speeding toward the town of Marina (on the outskirts of the Monterey Peninsula), he was oblivious to a train bearing down on the railroad crossing he was approaching. Upon rounding a bend near the crossing, he was jolted back to reality by blasts from the train's horn Frantically slamming on the brakes, he held his breath as the car skidded to a stop only inches from the moving train. Years later, when he told me about the incident, he spoke in hushed tones as he mentioned how he could feel the vibrations of the train as it passed him by. Sitting in the driver's seat with his hands still locked on the wheel, the man counted his blessings and said a prayer of thanks.

With the train continuing on its way, the shaken driver once again pointed his vehicle toward Monterey. Upon reaching his house (which he shared with his mother), he parked the car and went inside. As he quietly made his way toward the rear of the dwelling, he heard sobbing sounds coming from the living room. Entering the darkened room, he found his mother huddled in a chair and asked why she was crying. With a sob of relief his mother gave him a heart-

felt hug and told him about a terrible dream she had had . . .
a dream in which he had been killed by a train! So realistic
was the dream that the distraught lady had called her
daughter at one-thirty in the morning and insisted she contact the people in Watsonville her son had been visiting to
see whether he was all right.

## An allegedly haunted building . . .

Approximately twenty miles from Monterey is the community of Salinas. Known especially as the birthplace of John
Steinbeck, the valley town (like many older communities)
also boasts an interesting collection of ghostly tales. Among
them is the story of a mysterious presence, said to resemble
the famed author, that has been seen at Steinbeck's boyhood home (see "The feeling of presence mysteriously
vanished," page 77, and "The ghost of John Steinbeck,"
page 78).

This account takes us outside Salinas proper, to an
allegedly haunted building on the Monterey-Salinas road
(slightly south of the sprawling community). The tale was
told to me by two teachers who were taking a college extension course I was teaching. Among the happenings
reported at this house were strange and unidentifiable
sounds that were heard in different parts of the building,
cold spots that were felt in various rooms, and a number of
episodes involving "feelings of presence." What makes this
tale more interesting than most is information that states
the structure was once a nunnery . . . and that several of its
devout occupants had experienced the strange phenomena.

## He froze in his tracks . . .

I learned of this story while thumbing through an aged
scrapbook that had been put together by a Pacific Grove old-

timer. Included in the book were letters from local residents that had been printed in the *Monterey Peninsula Herald.* Several of the letters dealt with ghosts and mysterious happenings, one of which took place north of Salinas, in an area known as The Rocks. Already rich in legends of bandit lore, stagecoach robberies, and hidden treasures, the area became even better known with the addition of this ghostly tale.

The story takes us back to a storm-wracked night in 1933, as a Monterey motorist (who later wrote the letter) approached The Rocks. (In the early 1930s the road leading through the Rocks area was little more than a narrow strip of concrete.) Suddenly, as he neared a sharp turn in the midst of the massive rock formation, the lights from his automobile illuminated his pet dog. The animal seemed to know he was coming, and it rushed toward the car as if to force it to stop. Surprised and bewildered, the driver screeched to a halt. Braving the wind and rain, he jumped from his vehicle and followed the dog around the bend. It was then that he froze in his tracks. Not only had the dog vanished, but blocking the road was a huge truck and trailer lying on its side! The driver indicated that because of the stormy conditions, and the speed at which he had been traveling, he wouldn't have been able to avoid crashing into the truck. But what makes this story of interest to ghost enthusiasts is the fact that the dog, which had appeared out of nowhere, had died three months before!

## Wild-eyed and greatly disturbed . . .

A second letter from the *Monterey Peninsula Herald's* "ghostly file" (see preceding note) describes several strange occurrences at an old Carmel dwelling. How and why the incidents took place are open questions. As the letter points out, there were special circumstances preceding both the beginning and ending of the events.

Prior to the first of the strange happenings an elderly resident of the house died. Upon her death the four individuals who still lived in the building began hearing a number of "alarming" noises. These noises were described as sounding like someone was "angrily striking pieces of furniture." Although the sounds originated in the dark of night, they would persist even after the lights were turned on. When the structure was checked in the light of day, no sign of what caused the nighttime sounds could be found.

With this strange phenomenon continuing on a nightly basis, the daytime hours also began to be interrupted by an odd occurrence. A lone sparrow began arriving each morning at a living room window. After pecking at a certain window pane, it would fly away, only to return the next day at the same time, as if on a rigid mid-morning schedule. The sparrow always chose the same window pane, and arrived and departed as reliably as a factory worker punching a time clock.

During this unsettling period, a guest was housed in the deceased woman's room. Unfortunately, in the middle of the night the wild-eyed and greatly disturbed guest hastily vacated the room—and the building! As he departed he told his hosts he thought the room was haunted. Through chattering teeth he said he had been kept awake by "peculiar knockings, whackings, and other fearful noises." Curiously, approximately one week after the guest's sudden departure, a small sparrow, similar to the bird that had pecked its monotonous message on the window pane, was found dead at the front door.

What connection was there between the dead sparrow, the nightly banging, and the haunted bedroom? No one knows . . . but from that time on there were no alarming noises, no ghostly happenings, and no window-pecking sparrows at the Carmel cottage.

# The door was found locked from within . . .

Nestled in the heart of Carmel's quaint business district (and only a short walk from the cottage discussed in the last note) is a building that has long been a part of old Carmel. As mentioned in my book *Ghostly Tales and Mysterious Happenings of Old Monterey*, this historic structure has been the scene of several strange happenings. According to some of the town's old-timers, the sights, sounds, smells, and unexplained occurrences within the building are nothing to be concerned about. They merely nod and blame the odd events on the original owner, whose ghost is said to frequent the premises. Perhaps, as some have suggested, the spirit of this long-dead Carmelite has chosen to "stick around" and help the village retain the charm and beauty it has become noted for.

Here I would like to add a couple of incidents to those described in *Ghostly Tales*. The first account has baffled workers in the building for many years. As the story is told by a past manager of the popular retail outlet that occupies the site, one day the upstairs bathroom door was found locked from within. The lock was a spring-clasped hook that could be latched only from the inside. With a growing number of people desiring to use the facility, several fruitless attempts were made to persuade whoever was in the room to unlock the door. Finally the manager decided to try to enter the facility from the outside. A ladder was obtained and carefully positioned in a tiny courtyard in the center of the building. After gingerly making a climb of considerable height, the manager reached the partially stuck bathroom window. With considerable effort, the window was forced open and the manager squeezed through. The spring-clasped hook had indeed been securely fastened from within—but the room itself was empty!

A second unexplained incident is worthy of mention, if only because it adds to the long list of happenings that have taken place in the structure. Like the first, it happened in the upstairs section of the rambling old building. The original owner had an apartment in the back (it was near this room that the deceased owner's ghostly voice had once been heard in conversation with the famed author Jack London, an early visitor to old Carmel). As the story goes, a trusted employee of the business that occupied the back of the building was alone in the upstairs section when she heard several mysterious noises, followed by the sound of a window being shut. Concerned as to what was going on, the employee bravely entered the room from which the noises came. Though no one was there, the window had in fact been closed! Adding to her concern was the knowledge that considerable force was needed to shut the window, which had a history of being stuck. The lady ended her brief account by saying that while she stared at the window, feeling "most uncomfortable" in the room, the lights began to flicker! Needless to say, she made a hasty exit from the room, and from the upstairs section of the building . . .

# More Ghosts
## (1977–1990)

Most of the preceding incidents were documented during the early to mid-1970s, interspersed between the more than seventy-five accounts that were used in my first two ghost books. The remainder of the tales in this book are a selection of the ghost notes I recorded between January 1977 and June 1990, presented in the order I learned of them. Although most of them are entirely new stories, I have included a few that provide additional detail or confirmation of incidents reported earlier. Nearly all are published here for the first time.

# The aroma of roses . . .

*January 2, 1977*   A respected and well-known Monterey Peninsula resident* started 1977 off with a bang (as far as ghostly tales are concerned) when he shared a number of Robert Louis Stevenson House accounts with me. It seems that over a period of years this gentleman had become fascinated with the building and the number of ghost stories connected with it. This fascination prompted him to spend a considerable amount of time at the Stevenson House. After getting to know some of the workers and gaining their trust, he was given permission to roam the building at will during working hours.

It was during these visits, when he was alone in the upstairs section, that he experienced several odd occurrences. Among the happenings were sounds of furniture being moved. Upon checking, he reported, he found that furniture (whose location he had previously marked) had—indeed—been moved! Other sounds that he heard were footsteps in the upstairs hall, when no one was there to make them. Also of interest were lights that flickered and became very bright—almost to the bursting point; a stopped clock that suddenly started ticking and chiming; the aroma of roses in the hall and on the staircase (there were no roses in the building); and the movement of toys in the nursery (whose positions he had previously marked).

# A white flash darted down the hall . . .

*March 4, 1977*   After hearing my talk at one of Fort Ord's elementary schools, a teacher introduced herself and asked if I was the person who wrote the ghost stories. I admitted that I was, and she proceeded to tell me that she thought she had seen a ghost at the Robert Louis Stevenson House.

* Now deceased.

28

The incident took place in December of 1975, when she was visiting the building with a group of fourth- and fifth-grade boys. As the group listened to the guide at the entrance of one of the upstairs rooms, the teacher—out of the corner of her eye—saw a white flash dart down the hall and disappear around a corner. Thinking the blur was her "number one" troublemaker (who happened to be wearing a white shirt), she immediately gave chase. On rounding the corner she found herself at the entrance of the sewing room, which, after a quick inspection, revealed no people. Upon returning to her class, feeling bewildered about where her "problem child" could have gone, the shaken teacher saw the lad she was thinking about standing with the group and intent on what the guide was saying. Feeling foolish about her pursuit of something that wasn't there, and guilty about blaming the white flash on her innocent student, the teacher sheepishly told the curator about her experience. Nodding knowingly, the guide suggested that perhaps something strange *was* going on. Several other visitors, the guide told the teacher, had also reported seeing flashes of white!

## No one admits to having set it up . . .

*March 22, 1977*   As with Monterey's Robert Louis Stevenson House, strange tales about the Royal Presidio Chapel's old rectory continue to surface. A local teacher shared this brief tale with me. It seems that a complete place setting has frequently been found at the rectory's aged dining room table. However, no one admits to having set it up—and no one is known to have ever used it.

## Questions of who, how, and why . . .

*April 26, 1977*   The Robert Louis Stevenson House complex is made up of two adjoining structures. For many years

29

employees of the California Department of Parks and Recreation lived in the second (rear) building. A series of incidents were reported by one of the rangers who resided in these quarters. On more than one occasion, he said, he was awakened in the middle of the night by the sounds of an upstairs back door being opened. The door led from Stevenson's bedroom to a balcony that linked the two structures. Of added interest is the fact that the door was always opened from the inside. These events took place after the building had been checked and secured for the night. The questions of who, how, and why remain unanswered, and only add to the many mysteries of this historic structure.

## They matter-of-factly blamed them on the building's ghosts . . .

*August 1, 1977*   Among Monterey's many historic structures is the Merritt House. Located at 386 Pacific Street, this aged adobe has an interesting history. In the mid-1800s it was the home of Josiah Merritt, who helped with the organization of Monterey County and was one of its first judges. Over the years a number of odd occurrences are said to have taken place within the dwelling. Among the happenings reported were cabinet doors opening, latches becoming undone, water in the upstairs half-bath starting to run, and a toilet flushing when no one was in the bathroom. These events were told to me by a woman who once lived in the house for a short time. She went on to say that the owners of the dwelling were aware of the happenings and matter-of-factly blamed them on the building's ghosts.*

---

*Other strange occurrences at the Merritt House were later listed in an October 1977 issue of the *Monterey Peninsula Herald*. They included doors that slipped their locks, footsteps that were heard on the staircase, and noises that came from a variety of unlikely places. As would be expected, there was never anyone around to account for these happenings.

# And then he heard a heavy thud . . .

*August 8, 1977* A trusted friend told me this account involving the Royal Presidio Chapel. My friend heard it from the priest who experienced it.

One night, the priest said, he was in a side room of the church (where robes and assorted other items are kept), making sure things were in order for a 6:00 a.m. mass. Suddenly the silence was broken by the sounds of footsteps coming down the center aisle of the church. As the priest quietly listened, the footsteps stopped, and then he heard a heavy thud, "like somebody [was] dumping a body on the floor." The priest rushed from the room to see what was going on—only to find that there was no one in the church, and nothing on the floor.

# A sick man had lived there once . . .

*September 28, 1977* The schoolteacher who experienced the following happening at the Robert Louis Stevenson House was still in awe when she told me about it. A specialist in teaching children with learning difficulties, she frequently worked with students on a small group or individual basis. In working with a ten-year-old boy who showed an interest in things of long ago, the teacher decided that a trip to Monterey's historic buildings would be beneficial. With permission granted, the trip was made.

A second student was included in the outing, and the little group made a stop at the Stevenson House. As they were visiting the upstairs section, the boy for whom the trip was planned became excited about the rooms and the furnishings they contained. Talking as if he was very much aware of the people and events associated with this house of history, he proceeded to describe many of the objects that he saw and to tell about some of the things that had taken place within the rooms. Overwhelmed by his inexplicable

31

knowledge, and his sudden spark of enthusiasm, the teacher found it difficult to believe all that she was hearing.

When the threesome reached the children's nursery, the dumbfounded teacher became even more amazed as the boy seemed to be "in touch" with long-ago inhabitants of the room. Finally, "after coming back to reality," but still gazing into the nursery, the boy told his teacher about two children who had once stayed in the room (bringing to mind the previously told tale of Mrs. Girardin's grandchildren). Robert Louis Stevenson enthusiasts will be interested in knowing that upon leaving the nursery and seeing the Stevenson bedroom, the lad began talking about a sick man who had once lived there. (Stevenson himself was quite sick during the time he stayed in the structure.)

The questions of how the young boy knew so much about the building and its inhabitants of long ago remain unanswered. These questions become even more perplexing when one learns that the boy was a non-reader and that he had never before been to downtown Monterey.


## The dog went straight to Peggy's grave . . .

*September 29, 1977* Some time ago a lady I will call Peggy was having a late dinner with a friend in a waterside Moss Landing restaurant. (Moss Landing is a picturesque harbor community on Monterey Bay's east shore.) The night was warm, and the restaurant's door had been left open for ventilation. Suddenly, out of the night, a small black dog wandered into the restaurant and sought out Peggy. The animal was young, thin, hungry, and apparently abandoned. Although Peggy did not consider herself an "animal person," she couldn't find it in her heart to turn the dog away. Upon leaving the restaurant she took the animal home and cared for it. Soon the two were inseparable.

Several months later Peggy became ill, and within the year she died. During the time she was sick, the dog was her constant companion. However, when the end came, it disappeared. As time went on, the animal was all but forgotten.

About six months later, two of Peggy's friends were at the Salinas cemetery looking for grave sites. (The cemetery is not far from Peggy's old house.) While they were at the graveyard, the man in charge—a mutual friend who had also known Peggy—mentioned that approximately one week after Peggy died a black dog began appearing at the cemetery office each day at about the same time. After a while it would wander off, always heading in the same direction. Curious as to where it went, the man decided to follow it. To his surprise the dog went straight to Peggy's grave, where it lay down. After asking around, he was told by various workers that the dog came to the cemetery every day and spent most of its time lying on that one particular grave. Nearly two weeks later, the man saw the animal's body near the cemetery gate—the victim of a car accident.

With the dog's death ending the story, I mentioned to the person who was telling me this tale (a long-time friend) that it was a rather sad ending. But she disagreed, stating that in her opinion it was a happy ending, since Peggy and her dog were together again.

## His ghostly presence tried to keep them out . . .

*September 30, 1977* Although Monterey is best known for its adobes (buildings made of sun-dried bricks of clay and straw), it also boasts several historic structures of other kinds. Among them is the Perry House, locally known as Monterey's first Victorian. Located on the southeast corner of Van Buren and Scott streets, the building was constructed by Manuel Perry in the 1860s. Perry is thought by some to have been the captain of a whaling vessel. (Monterey was the hub of a shore-whaling industry that began in 1854.)

Over the years the Perry House has undergone several changes and additions. Among the stories that have been told about the building is the tale of an unfriendly ghost. This account, which has circulated among Montereyans for several years, indicates that long ago a lady was killed in one of the upstairs rooms. Ironically, the ghost is not the lady, but rather the man who killed her. For a period of time after the man's death his ghost is said to have haunted the room in which the killing took place. Whenever anyone tried to enter the room, his ghostly presence would try to keep them out—to the extent of chasing the intruder down the stairs! Happily for those who currently frequent the building, the ghost has not been seen for many years, and today the attractive old Victorian radiates a feeling of warmth and charm.

## They heard rumbling noises . . .

*October, 1977*  The October 1977 issue of the Monterey Peninsula's *This Month* magazine carried an article entitled "Oh, There's a Ghost at Stevenson House," by El Frieda and Herbert Liese. Included in the story was information about two happenings that had been experienced by the building's gardener.

This highly educated and multitalented man had worked at the facility for twenty years. During his tenure he turned the gardens into a showplace of old Monterey. The first of his experiences took place early one morning before the building, and its enclosed rear gardens, were open to visitors. While he was on his knees working among the flowers, he heard the sounds of approaching footsteps. Thinking the gate had been opened for visitors to await the building's first tour, he didn't even bother to look up from his work. However, as the footsteps came to a stop, he noticed a pair of men's shoes (topped with green trousers) by his side. Expecting to see an inquisitive visitor, the gardener looked up and was amazed to discover that not only was there no one there, but there wasn't a soul in the entire garden! Bewildered, the gardener jumped to his feet and looked around the corner of the building, half-expecting to see a fleet-footed fellow disappearing from sight. Of course, there was no one to be seen . . .

The second strange happening experienced by the gardener took place inside the building.* After he returned from the community of Gilroy (approximately 42 miles north of Monterey) with a load of original Stevenson House furnishings, a number of the items were placed upstairs. Early the next morning, when only he, the curator, and a cleaning lady were in the building, they heard rumbling noises coming from a room directly above them. As they listened, it became obvious that the sounds were being made by a heavy object being dragged across the floor. An immediate check of the upstairs section revealed nary a soul, nor anything out of place! It has since been suggested that the Stevenson House ghost disapproved of the placement of the newly acquired furniture and chose this way to let his (or her) concerns be known.

## Electricity and sparks emanated from him . . .

*February 6, 1978*   On February 6, 1978, an article appeared in the *Monterey Peninsula Herald*, telling about several ghostly happenings that took place at a Monterey liquor store. The story aroused considerable local interest when it was published and was soon picked up by a national tabloid. Knowing the *Herald* reporter who wrote the original article, and knowing a little about the building's background, I too became interested in the account. I was par-

---

*I have described similar events in other publications, but I think this account is worthy of mention, as it adds credence to the earlier tales.

ticularly interested in a ghostly apparition that appeared to a lady who had been placed under hypnosis by a parapsychologist who had been called in to investigate the events. The parapsychologist was well known throughout central California and had investigated several haunted buildings.

In describing the apparition that she saw, the lady said "he" was in an upstairs corner, "and appeared to have electricity and sparks emanating from him." While there was more to her account, it was the mention of electricity and sparks that caught my attention (she even referred to the apparition as the "electric man"). A little more than ten years before this event took place, a man—referred to by some as an electrical genius—was killed in the building while working on an invention. With this thought in mind, I couldn't help but wonder whether the "electric man" observed by the lady while under hypnosis was the spirit of the inventor . . . who once ran the electric shop within the structure, who was a pioneer in the field of electrical radiant heating, and who tragically met death—in the building in question—while devising a method to take the wrinkles out of prunes.

## Unseen things go up and down the stairs . . .

*February 15, 1978*  I was chatting with a local schoolteacher, and our conversation soon got around to the delightful Carmel dwelling she lives in. However, in discussing the house she began to bemoan the fact that—as charming as the structure is—she has had little luck renting it out during the summer, when she travels and visits family and friends. I was curious what the problem might be, since I felt the dwelling would be a desirable summer rental, so I asked how much she rented the house for. The problem, she replied, wasn't getting renters—it was keeping them! With that she proceeded to tell me about some of the strange happenings that have taken place in the structure, such as the washer and dryer turning on and off by themselves and

36

mysterious "people sounds" being heard as unseen things go up and down the stairs! "On numerous occasions," she concluded, "after renting the house and traveling about, I would receive word that my summer guests had vacated the premises due to the ghostly happenings that took place."

## The clicking sounds followed them . . .

*March, 1978*  A family that visited Carmel Mission reported having a strange experience in the courtyard of the church. While looking around the front garden area in the company of their pet dog, they began hearing a series of clicking sounds. As the sounds became louder—indicating that whatever was making them was getting closer—the family began to become alarmed. The most frightened of all was the dog, which whimpered and whined, tugging on its leash in an effort to get away. Thinking the dog had the right idea, the family decided to return to their car. Unfortunately, the clicking sounds followed them! However, upon reaching the security of the automobile, the dog suddenly became brave and barked ferociously as it jumped from seat to seat in a frantic effort to follow the sounds, which had begun to circle the vehicle. Only after they had driven away from the mission did the clicking sounds cease.

This account brings to mind various tales of the ghost of an aged Peninsula priest that has been seen in the mission's front court. The priest is known to have had a dog, and people who are familiar with these stories wonder whether the clicking sounds were made by the deceased priest's pet in an effort to let the intruding animal know it was treading on his turf.

## A haunted hillside mansion . . .

*April, 1978*  In Carmel there is a hillside mansion that has had a remarkable history. To this day the building remains a house of mystery and intrigue. Situated approximately halfway between Carmel's main street (Ocean Avenue) and its historic mission, the mansion lies at the end of a long, narrow driveway and overlooks California's famed El Camino Real, the two-century-old "King's Highway" that connected Spain's Alta California missions. Partly because it is hidden from view, and partly because rumors have circulated about it for more than half a century, the stately old structure has acquired an almost indescribable mystique. Among other things, the building is said to have been used as a rum-runner's haven during Prohibition (complete with a secret room to hide the booze) and is referred to by old-timers as a house where "strange things happen."

Many of the odd occurrences that have taken place in the building have been related to me by respected and reliable Carmel residents, including city administrators and policemen. The stories include traditional ghostly happenings, such as the movement of objects from their proper places and their mysterious return at a later date. Other tales include stories pertaining to the building's heavy hardwood doors. The more common of these accounts tell of upstairs doors that are found open in the morning, after having been shut and checked the night before. Moreover, certain doors have been known to suddenly swing open— and just as suddenly slam shut. When happenings such as these have occurred, the building has immediately been checked for open windows or doors that could have caused a draft, but none have ever been found. Still another tale relates how some of the doors that had been purposely left unlocked would—at most inopportune times—be found locked, almost as if a mischievous ghost were playing a trick.

It's not only the doors that seem to be toys for unseen hands. Several people have witnessed another unusual happening: the movement of fireplace tools, which are made of wrought iron and topped with silver handles. For no apparent reason—again, no windows or doors were open to create a draft—the tools would start to swing when no one was near them. Also unique to this building is the unpredictable action of certain window shades, which have the habit of slamming down—not up!

Over the years many other tales have been told about the house. According to one of the most interesting stories, several years ago a well-known local man and his family were thinking about moving into the mansion. While they were attempting to make up their minds, other family matters and concerns came into their lives. Among them was the question of whether they should buy a new car. The new car issue became quite heated, with opinions varying from "Yes, the old car is unsafe!" to "No, we can't afford a new car!" One night, as the discussion once again heated up, tempers became short, and the man of the house decided that taking time out might help to clear the air.

Jumping into the family car, he began to drive around aimlessly, lost in thought and unaware of where he was going. Before long he "came back to reality" and realized he was in front of the Monterey cemetery. Thinking this would be as good a place as any to take a walk and attempt to sort things out, he parked the car and began to wander through the graveyard. Suddenly, he heard an "inner voice" telling him to stop. Obeying this somewhat frightening command, he stopped and uneasily glanced around. Although it was difficult to see clearly in the dead of night, he realized that he was in a part of the cemetery he had never visited before. Feeling out of place, and more than a little uncomfortable, he glanced at the tombstone he had stopped in front of. To his shock, he discovered that he was standing squarely in front of the grave of the person whose ghost was said to haunt the hillside mansion—the very house he was thinking of moving into! Badly shaken by this experience, the man wasted little time bidding adieu to the Monterey cemetery.

In ending this account I must add that while driving back to his Carmel home, the man thought about how his visit to the graveyard might have been an omen. Perhaps, he reasoned, in some strange way he was being warned that death and unsafe cars go hand in hand. With this in mind he decided that maybe the family could afford a new car after all. He came to one other decision as well. Even though his walk through the graveyard had helped him make what might have been a life-saving decision, it also convinced him that he was not the type of person who would be comfortable living in a haunted mansion!

## The cold spot engulfed an entire room . . .

*April 21, 1978*   Four people and a dog can't be wrong . . . At least that was the opinion of the occupants of a turn-of-the-century Pacific Grove dwelling. Perhaps, they mused, if there had been only one witness to the strange happenings in the house, the person would have had a difficult time convincing the others. But with all of them experiencing the odd occurrences, they had little choice but to agree that they shared the house with an unseen thing. The happenings included objects falling from the wall and almost striking people; the front door opening and slamming shut by itself; footsteps heard bounding up the stairs, as well as in upstairs rooms, when no one was in the house to account for them; a cold spot that engulfed an entire room that had once been warm and cheerful; and—the most unnerving of all—the behavior of their dog, which barked at an invisible presence and refused to go upstairs . . .

## The house snaps and pops . . .

*April 24, 1978*   Here is an unusual story. An aged redwood house in Carmel has a habit of snapping and popping when certain people are mentioned—or even thought about! According to the wife of a well-known Carmelite, when the conversation gets around to her deceased parents, the house snaps and pops "all over the place." When the conversation stops, so does the snapping and popping. On occasion, when she has been deep in thought about her parents, the house also has snapped and popped. Various people have been in the structure when these happenings have occurred, and all are bewildered witnesses to the strange sounds.

## She felt a gentle "hit" on her shoulder . . .

*September 13, 1978* A house on Monterey's Van Buren Street is said to contain the ghost of a man attired in "an old-fashioned coat." According to the woman who told me this tale, his image has only been seen by a couple of people, but the noises he makes, and the activities attributed to him, have been experienced by many more. Among the happenings experienced by a girl who once lived there was a gentle "hit" on her shoulder. The tap did not hurt her, but it was strong enough to convince her a presence was there. Unfortunately for the owners of this aged dwelling, they have a difficult time keeping it rented because of the supernatural happenings that are associated with it.

## The building mysteriously collapsed . . .

*October 10, 1978* After a talk I gave in downtown Monterey, a member of the audience told me a sad tale about a child who lost her life in a local fire. The building the child was in at the time of the blaze was also lost to the hungry flames. After the debris was cleared away, repeated attempts were made to construct a second building on the site of the first. However, for unknown reasons all of the construction attempts failed, as each time the building began to take shape it mysteriously collapsed!

## Brief and to the point . . .

*October 10, 1978* A popular Monterey Peninsula priest also had a comment for me after my talk (see preceding note). My session included a number of stories relating to ghosts, so it was appropriate for similar tales to be told. Still, I was surprised and delighted to hear his comment, as it reaffirmed a story I had heard previously (see "A long-dead priest," page 16). Brief and to the point, the priest said he also knew the famous historian who had told me about seeing the ghost of his priest friend, and that the historian had told him about this sighting.

## In the dark of the moon . . .

*October, 1978* An article in the October 1978 issue of *This Month* magazine discusses a large rock wall in Carmel. The property enclosed by the wall is bounded by Guadalupe, Santa Rita, Fourth, and Fifth streets. Stories have circulated about this area since the wall was constructed in the 1920s. One of the accounts mentioned in the article tells of hoofbeats that are heard "in the dark of the moon." Supposedly, the haunted hoofbeats are those of a horse that long ago fell into a well near the north wall.

## The presence radiated a warm and friendly feeling . . .

*March 6, 1979* Seventeenth Street in Pacific Grove is well known for its Victorian structures. It is in one of these buildings that this story takes place. Upon moving into the house in question an older woman and her daughter spent the first night sleeping on the floor. During the night the mother woke up to the sounds of footsteps in the hall heading toward the bathroom. Thinking it was her daughter, she lay awake waiting for her to return. Soon she heard footsteps approaching the room they were in, but when they reached the door they stopped. Concerned, the mother got up to investigate. It was then that she noticed her daughter asleep in her sleeping bag, where she had been the entire time. A quick check of the hall revealed nary a clue as to who (or what) had made the sounds.

Another "clueless" happening that took place in the house was the feeling of someone—or something—sitting on a bed. On one such occasion, when the mother was resting, she felt the bed give as if someone had sat down beside her. Thinking it was her daughter, she turned to give her a hug . . . but no one was there! Upon learning of this incident, the daughter had a difficult time accepting it until a similar experience happened to her. One day, after lying down to take a nap, the younger woman felt her bed give as if someone had sat on it. Thinking it was her mother, she opened her eyes to find no one on the bed—or anywhere in the room.

In sharing these incidents with me, the older woman insisted that the happenings were not scary. Instead, she said, the presence radiated a warm and friendly feeling, as if it was happy with the way the house was being cared for.


## The ghostly figure was an Indian princess . . .

*May 19, 1979* After hearing a talk I gave to a group of ladies in Carmel Valley, an elderly woman matter-of-factly stated that the ghostly figure seen climbing the rear steps of an aged Cachagua ranch house (as described in my book *Ghostly Tales and Mysterious Happenings of Old Monterey*) was that of an Indian princess. (The Cachagua section of Carmel Valley is approximately 20 miles east of the main valley entrance.)

The woman's mention of the ranch house, which was

built in the late 1800s, was of interest to me, since twice before (in 1973 and 1976) I have heard ghost stories connected with it. A second incident (also discussed in *Ghostly Tales*) tells of a presence that was sensed by the family dog in the living room. The happening usually occurred at night as the two occupants of the house were relaxing with their pet dog before a cozy fire. Suddenly the dog would wake up from a deep sleep and stare across the room. With its eyes wide, the hair on its back raised, and its nose quivering, the dog would whimper and whine as it continued to stare across the room. The couple were never able to find anything out of place, or see a presence of any kind. However, upon crossing the room to where the dog stared, they passed through a cold spot—even though the rest of the room had been warmed by the fire! (For those unfamiliar with tales of the supernatural, a cold spot is often described as a place where spirits enter or exit a building.)

## The sound of the door slamming echoed in her ears...

*May 26, 1979*   While enjoying a cup of coffee at a Carmel cafe, I heard another story relating to the village's haunted hillside mansion (see "A haunted hillside mansion," page 37). In the presence of several friends, including a number of city administrators, the woman who was living in the house at the time acknowledged that many ghostly happenings took place there, and enthusiastically added one of her own.

Occurrences such as creaking floors and assorted other sounds were rather common in the house, the woman told us, but one day she heard another noise that scared the daylights out of her. While she was alone in the house, busy with her chores, the distinct sounds of footsteps drifted down from the attic. Hoping (and praying) that the sounds were just another of the many odd occurrences that took

44

place in the building, the lady managed to remain some-what calm and collected for approximately fifteen minutes. It was then that she heard an upstairs door slam shut! The sound of the door slamming echoed in her ears as she ran from the house, jumped in her car, and sped to the police station. Converging on the scene, the police searched the house, but didn't find anyone on the premises, or anything missing or out of place.

After only a moment's hesitation, the lady followed with a second short account. The next day, she continued, when her teenage son came home from school, he dropped some bread in the toaster and prepared to make a snack. However, as he waited for the toast to pop up, he heard heavy foot-steps from upstairs! Knowing the house was supposed to be empty, he bolted for the door—not even waiting for his after-noon snack.

## He glimpsed a ghostly galleon . . .

*June 26, 1979* The Pebble Beach area of the Monterey Peninsula is noted for its world-famous golf courses, the scenic Seventeen Mile Drive, wind-swept cypress trees, long-ago shipwrecks, and magnificent ocean view homes. It is in one of these aged, exotic, and multilevel homes that this story begins.

As related by the man who experienced it, early one morning (about 1:00 a.m.), as he was asleep in the huge Pebble Beach house, he was awakened by the sounds of a fierce Pacific storm, accompanied by dreadful feelings of fear and icy cold. Even though he was a visitor to the area and alone in the structure, it wasn't the sounds of the storm that bothered him. He had experienced many such storms, both at sea and on land, and the sounds of crashing waves, moaning trees, creaking houses, and gale-force winds didn't concern him. What did bother him were his frighten-ing feelings and the bitter cold. Not knowing what caused the feelings, and becoming more alarmed as they became more intense, he jumped from his bed and began a frantic search of the dwelling. Making his way from room to room, becoming more aware of his feelings as he went, he began to wonder if the house was haunted and if some horrible happening had taken place there, perhaps at the height of a raging storm. Finally, he completed the search without finding anything out of place or experiencing any unnatural happenings. As he stepped outside to look around the yard, however, his feelings of fear and intense cold became even stronger and seemed to be drawing him toward the sea. Walking almost trancelike toward the shore, he felt as if he was reliving a scene of long ago, a scene that included a tragic shipwreck and the loss of many lives. Stopping amid the rocks and sand of the nearby beach, he gazed out to sea and seemed to glimpse a ghostly galleon foundering in the storm-wracked water. To make the scene all the more realistic, he thought he could hear the anguished cries of the crew as they pitted their strength against the sea in futile attempts to reach the safety of shore.

After recounting this event in considerable detail, the man mentioned that the story may not be over yet. At some future date, he said, he hopes to dive in the area to see whether he can find any evidence of a long-ago shipwreck. His search may not be in vain. According to local residents, many years ago the unidentified figurehead of an ancient sailing vessel washed ashore on a nearby beach.

## He was afraid to go into the room alone . . .

*July, 1979*  The structure known as Monterey's Whaling Station, located in the Heritage Harbor complex near Fisherman's Wharf, was built in the 1840s by David Wight, an adventurer from England. While somewhat similar to many of Monterey's Spanish-style buildings, it was also unique in a number of ways, one of them being that it faced north (toward the bay), rather than east (toward the rising sun)—a fact that helped shape its destiny. Even though Wight constructed the building as a home for his family, it wasn't long before they were bitten by the gold bug and headed for California's Mother Lode. However, the dwelling didn't remain empty for long. In the mid-1850s members of the Old Monterey Whaling Company (also known as the "Old Company") occupied the structure. Since the Wight house overlooked Monterey Bay, it served as an ideal headquarters for the whalers. According to Monterey legend, lookouts maintained a vigil at the upstairs windows, where they could spot the mammoth creatures frolicking in the bay.

Other, more recent, stories tell of ghostly happenings that have taken place in the historic structure. I learned some of these tales from a concerned, and somewhat frightened, man whose job it was to keep an eye on the building. After giving me a call and sharing a few of the happenings, he asked whether I could meet him at the Station and try to help him figure out what was going on. The fact that I wasn't a professional ghost hunter didn't concern him, so I hurried to my car and headed for the bayside building. After being given a bit of background, I was escorted through the facility. As he showed me around, the man told me that he had experienced several of the happenings—in the company of others—the night before. Among these events was an overwhelming feeling of presence in several of the rooms. The rooms in question included a downstairs front room (to the right of the main entrance), an upstairs bedroom (where the feeling was strongest near the fireplace), and the upstairs bathroom (where a "frightening feeling" was experienced). However, the most frightening feeling of all was in what the man described as the upstairs locker room. It was this room that he was afraid to go into alone.

As we toured the facility, the man also mentioned cold spots that had followed him through the building, even though many of the happenings had taken place on a warm July night. In a downstairs room my escort pointed to curtains that had flowed toward him when the doors and windows were shut and the building was void of breezes. In concluding, the man said that when he and a fellow worker experienced some of the odd occurrences, the hair on their arms rose, and they both boasted an extreme case of goose pimples.

As for me, I can't say I experienced anything out of the ordinary, but in defense of the gentleman who showed me around the building, he agreed that while I was there none of the peculiar happenings took place.

## Something terrible had happened where they were standing...

*July 15, 1979* Pacific Grove's Central Avenue is one of the main entrances into town and boasts many delightful Victorians. One of these dwellings, situated on a corner only a block from the bay, has an interesting history and is said to be haunted by a troubled spirit. A woman who had lived in the structure told of a number of strange happenings, including sounds that appeared to come from within the walls, "as if something were inside trying to get out." In attempting to describe the odd noises, she spoke of them as being "unhappy sounds." Also unhappy was one of the lady's teenage daughters, who complained of being pushed down a flight of stairs by an "unseen thing." On separate occasions, two people who visited the house suddenly indicated they felt uncomfortable, "as if something terrible had happened" where they were standing. In both cases these feelings were experienced in the downstairs living room, near the corner of a brick fireplace.

Apparently it wasn't only people who experienced peculiar feelings; the family's two dogs were similarly "spooked" by something they sensed in the house (or walls). The dogs also reacted negatively to the spot near the fireplace where the visitors had experienced the uncomfortable feelings. In closing, the lady said that the entire house seemed to be filled with tension, and her family was much happier after they moved from the dwelling.

## The candle was floating in the air . . .

*July 15, 1979* Late one night in the library of the old rectory next to Monterey's Royal Presidio Chapel, a young man was hard at work. Reported to be in his twenties, the man was studying to become a priest. While engrossed in his work, he heard a noise outside the door, which led to the inner hall. Thinking someone was there, he opened the door. To his shock all that could be seen was a brightly burning candle that appeared to be floating in the air about four feet off the floor. As the man stared in stunned silence, the candle remained still for a matter of seconds, and then fell to the floor! The experience was so unsettling to the young man that he refused to return to the library and soon left the area.

## Feelings of not being wanted . . .

*October 25, 1979* A few days before Halloween, I had occasion to spend a couple of hours with two friends (an artist from Carmel and a former policeman) in what was reported to be a haunted house in the Carmel Highlands. (The Carmel Highlands is a picturesque coastal community located just south of the Monterey Peninsula.) Perched high on a hill, the secluded house was spooky in appearance, especially at night (we arrived at about 9:00 p.m.). As we groped through the darkness, trying to find the front door, the spookiness of the scene was greatly enhanced by the mournful howling of a dog in the distance.

Upon locating the entrance, we (somewhat hesitatingly) explored the three levels of the house. After satisfying our curiosity and assuring ourselves that no one else was in the building, we attempted to make ourselves comfortable in the downstairs living room (unfortunately, the entire house was empty of furniture). As we sat on the floor waiting for something to happen, the ex-policeman, who had set up our visit, proceeded to tell us a little about the house and the lady who had it built. Said to date back to the 1920s, the structure was owned by a woman who was a friend or follower of the popular American evangelist Aimee Semple McPherson. Among the things that made the house special, aside from its dramatic ocean view, was a hidden passageway it was rumored to contain (which we were unable to find). As the policeman continued with his tales, we learned that the majority of the house's strange happenings occurred upstairs while the building's occupants were downstairs (thus explaining why he wanted us to remain downstairs). Among the happenings that had been experienced by several people were doors that opened and closed, lights that turned on and off, footsteps that were heard, and the sounds of heavy shoes or boots dropping to the floor. Needless to say, all these events took place when no one was upstairs to account for them. Past residents and visitors also told of feelings of "not being wanted" or of having "get out of the house" sensations. As for us, we didn't feel unwanted, but we did get out of the house (around 11:00 p.m.). Unfortunately for ghost enthusiasts, we had to admit that the only "sure thing" we got out of our visit was flea bites!

## There is no haunted house more famous . . .

*October 30, 1979*   The October 28, 1979, issue of the *Monterey Peninsula Herald's* "Weekend Magazine" carried an article entitled "Those Scary Ghosts Come Out on All Saints' Eve." Written by Bob Walch, the story contained several interesting ghostly tales, most of them from outside the Monterey Peninsula. However, those who discount the ghost stories connected with the Robert Louis Stevenson House might note the article's introductory paragraph: "Perhaps there is no haunted house more famous in Northern California . . . than the Stevenson House in Monterey."

The following incident should also be of interest to those who chalk the Robert Louis Stevenson House stories up to "recent" ghost hysteria (as some local residents are prone to do). After my Halloween Eve talk to a group of Monterey's senior citizens, a retired United States Army general was among those who came forward to thank me for the program and to share a few memories of their own. What makes the general's comments especially important was the information that the ghost stories connected with the Stevenson structure had been with us for, in his words, "quite a spell." In fact, he said, he had heard similar tales when he visited Monterey back in 1924! Stevenson House skeptics may wish to note that no matter how anyone looks at it, 1924 is hardly "recent" history.

## The rider was terrified to see fang-like teeth . . .

*December 13, 1979* This tale was told by a lady in her nineties, who proudly traces her heritage back to the earliest days of old Monterey. Among the stories she shared with a member of one of my college extension courses was one that boasts a variety of versions, and is well known to long-time Peninsulans.*

According to the woman's story, one evening many years ago her father was riding his horse toward home when he encountered a small child crying by the side of the road.

---

*A colorful, but very brief, version—telling of a laughing, squirming, fiendish red devil—is related in my book *Ghosts, Bandits and Legends of Old Monterey.*

51

Stopping his horse, the gallant gentleman dismounted to see whether he could be of help. With no one around, and with the child seemingly unwilling (or, perhaps, too young) to answer his questions, the rider decided to take him with him.

As they continued along the old wagon road, the child began to talk "in a strange way," indicating he wanted the rider to look in his mouth. Obliging his young companion, the man was terrified to see fang-like teeth! Thinking he had befriended the devil, the rider immediately rid himself of the "fiendish little fellow" and raced off into the night! Even though this tale may seem hard to believe, accounts similar to it have circulated around the Monterey Bay area for countless years.

## The sound of a woman moaning . . .

*December 18, 1979* Tragedy supposedly struck three times in a Carmel cottage near Fourth Street. The events took place in the 1920s and resulted in the death of two children and their mother. For several years after the tragedies occurred, the owner of the dwelling had a difficult time keeping it rented because of strange noises that were heard about the premises . . . including the sound of a woman moaning.

## Spirits in the rectory . . .

*December, 1979* A brief account from a local teacher concerning the old rectory of the Royal Presidio Chapel: Around the turn of the century, a priest who lived in the rectory talked about seeing spirits in the building and a rocking chair moving with no one in it.

## When he turned to face the candle holder . . .

*December 24, 1979*  On this day before Christmas I was given a newspaper clipping entitled "The Mission Haunt," by Richard L. Senate. (Unfortunately, the name and date of the paper were omitted.) The mission discussed was San Antonio, founded by Father Junipero Serra in 1771 and located in south Monterey County. San Antonio is one of the last of California's coastal missions to remain in its rural setting, and its church has been beautifully restored. Numerous strange stories are connected with the church.* The "Mission Haunt" article tells a fascinating story about an archaeology student who was doing field work at the mission. Along with several other students, he was housed in the mission complex. Late one night, after working in the museum, the student entered the inner courtyard and headed for his room. Across the garden, in an outer corridor, he saw someone carrying a candle and walking in the same direction he was. Thinking that this person was one of the Franciscan monks who lived at the mission, or perhaps another student, he continued toward his room. Reaching a far door at about the same time as the person carrying the candle, he stepped into the corridor to greet his fellow night owl. However, when he turned to face the candle holder, there was nothing to be seen!

## His presence creates a warm and friendly feeling . . .

*December 27, 1979*  Without a doubt one of the best-known streets on the Monterey Peninsula is Cannery Row. It

---

* A number of the tales, including an account of the famed "Headless Horsewoman," are in my book *Ghostly Tales and Mysterious Happenings of Old Monterey.*

was originally known as Ocean View Avenue and bordered a scenic section of the Monterey shore. However, as Monterey's sardine industry went into high gear during the 1920s, 30s, and early 40s, the bayside street became cluttered with fish canneries and reduction plants. Eventually the sardine disappeared from local waters, and the bustling activity that had once been a trademark of the street was no more. It was during this period, as Monterey's fishing industry began its decline, that John Steinbeck's popular novel *Cannery Row* was published (1945). With the book creating renewed interest in the area and Steinbeck fans flocking to the cannery-lined street, Monterey's city fathers changed the name of the street to Cannery Row. Unfortunately, by the time this took place (1953), many of the characters Steinbeck had written about—the people who helped make Cannery Row the colorful street that it was—were gone. Nevertheless, many of the aged buildings remained (at least those that hadn't succumbed to the numerous fires that ravaged the area). Today the Row is a totally different place, and many of those same buildings house restaurants and shops that cater to the throngs of visitors who continue to flock to the street. According to many tales, these old buildings also house a number of ghosts.

One such structure dates back to the earliest days of Cannery Row and played a prominent part in Steinbeck's book. The ghost that is most often observed in this building is that of an elderly Chinese gentleman. His image has been seen by numerous people. The ghost is described as "very inquisitive" and is thought by some to have been a chef or restaurant worker, since he has frequently been seen in the section of the building that once housed a popular cafe. His image has also been seen and heard (at least the shuffling of his slipper-like shoes) in the upstairs portion of the building. Despite the popular conception of ghosts as fearsome or evil, this ghostly presence does not transmit a scary feeling. Contrary to how many people think a "respectable" ghost should act, his presence is said to create a warm and friendly feeling.

# The figure disappeared into a wall . . .

*January 2, 1980*  I talked with another person who was familiar with Cannery Row's elderly Chinese ghost. For many years this person managed an art gallery that was located in a portion of the building the ghost was said to frequent (reportedly the same section of the building that contained the Cannery Row cafe mentioned in the preceding account). During her years in the gallery this woman heard a variety of ghostly sounds. The sound she remembered best was a "dull thud" that made her think of a body falling to the floor. The sound came from upstairs, when no one was in that part of the building. Later that same night, the hard-working lady saw the "shadowy figure" of a man emerge from the wall! After crossing the gallery, the figure (which she described as "small in stature") disappeared into a second wall.

Other upstairs noises the manager mentioned included the shuffling of slipper-like shoes (similar to sounds described in the preceding note). Another occurrence that baffled her took place near the rear of the facility, where two swinging (saloon-type) doors separated the front of the gallery from a small back room. Suddenly, and for no apparent reason, the doors began to violently swing back and forth. At the time this took place, there were no customers (or drafts) in the gallery.

Perhaps the most amazing event, however, occurred when the facility was closed and supposedly empty. Early one morning, the manager said, she arrived for work and found one whole wall of pictures on the floor face up. Not one picture, or frame, was damaged, and each item appeared to have been handled with care. In recounting this tale, the manager shook her head as if she was still in awe. No one, she stated emphatically, had been in the gallery, since when she arrived it was still locked, just as she had left it the night before!

# Sounds that turn to mournful cries . . .

*January, 1980*   As coincidence would have it, this note also involves Chinese ghosts. While reading the book *Ghost Towns of the Santa Cruz Mountains*, by John V. Young, I came across an account that hints of Chinese ghosts that may still haunt lonely canyons in the vicinity of an old railroad tunnel. Known to history buffs simply as "The Tunnel," it was located in the Santa Cruz Mountains near the small settlement of Wright's Station. According to the account, various sources indicated that between 17 and 200 Chinese workers were killed in a blast while working in the tunnel. Apparently, as was the case in other California locations, Chinese laborers in the Santa Cruz Mountains were not accorded the dignity of a formal count (thus the discrepancy in the number of dead.)

There are often similarities in ghost tales, as with other legends, even when they concern different times and places. This tale interests me because of certain similarities between it and a story I touched on in *Ghosts, Bandits and Legends of Old Monterey* (and documented, in a bit more detail, in *Incredible Ghosts of the Big Sur Coast*). Instead of a railroad tunnel in the Santa Cruz Mountains (north of Monterey Bay), my account involves a coal shaft in the Santa Lucia Mountains (south of Monterey Bay, near Carmel Highlands). The coal-shaft story involves somewhere between 40 and 70 Chinese coal miners (rather than railroad workers) who lost their lives, depending on which source one wishes to believe. The other main point of similarity is the hauntings themselves. In the Santa Cruz Mountains mishap, Chinese ghosts are said to haunt lonely canyons around the railroad tunnel to this day. Similarly, old-time Highlanders tell of eerie sounds they sometimes hear when Pacific winds blow up the canyons and play in the trees. These sounds turn to mournful cries, the Highlanders say, near the abandoned coal shaft . . . where the Chinese miners were buried alive.

# He was never seen again . . .

*January, 1980*  This tale was told to a teacher in one of my college extension courses and was presented as part of an "interviewing old-timers" project. The person who related the story was a woman in her eighties whose father had owned a popular mountain tavern on the old Mount Madonna Road north of Watsonville. Over the years a number of the tavern's customers boasted somewhat questionable reputations. Even the famed California badman Joaquin Murrieta is reported to have frequented the establishment. Among its more regular customers, however, was a young Watsonville man I will call Peter. Part of Peter's job was to deliver supplies to the tavern. While there he was known to take a nip or two before starting back down the mountain. Peter made a habit of leaving the premises long before night fell, and he was sometimes teased about being afraid of the dark. One afternoon, he was questioned by the bartender (the father of the woman who passed on this story) about why he always left so early. In response Peter confided that he had had several frightening experiences on the mountain road. Included in his bizarre tale was the description of a "headless traveler dressed in black" who had repeatedly stopped him as he made his way down the mountain. On each occasion the figure appeared at the same turn, where he would stand in the road "with outstretched arms." As Peter pulled his wagon to a stop, the traveler would climb aboard and ride part way down the mountain with him. Upon reaching a certain spot, the figure would indicate he wanted to get off. After Peter stopped, the traveler would climb down from the wagon and disappear into the woods.

One day, not long after Peter shared this story with the bartender, circumstances prevented him from getting his usual early start from the tavern. As the sun sank in the western sky, Peter realized he wouldn't be able to make it down the mountain before dark. In an attempt to bolster his courage he ordered himself a whiskey . . . and then another. As it turned out, it wasn't until several whiskies later that he felt ready to make the trip.

Perhaps the bartender had dismissed Peter's dread of going down the mountain at night. If so, it must have given him pause that after leaving the tavern neither Peter nor his horse or wagon was ever seen again! That Peter met with a grisly end can hardly be doubted, for hunters later reported finding his soiled and slashed clothing in a thicket near the base of the mountain.

## The fog created people-like shapes . . .

*January 24, 1980*  Among the many people I have had the pleasure of meeting while collecting ghost stories about the Monterey Peninsula was a delightful—if slightly eccentric—lady in Carmel. Not only was she a pleasure to talk to, but being able to visit her house (which has since been torn down) was a real treat for a history buff like me. Constructed in 1910, the building was said by some to have been the literary center of old Carmel. Among the writers she described as having visited the dwelling in the early years were Jack London, George Sterling, Sinclair Lewis, Fred Bechdoldt, Redfern Mason, Upton Sinclair, and Mary Austin.

While my acquaintance had much to tell me about the unique history of the house, she also had a ghostly tale to share that took place at a location nearby. Many years ago—long before Carmel became the tourist-oriented community it is today—she had left her house for a stroll through the forest. Proceeding in a southerly direction toward Carmel Mission (and following a portion of the previously mentioned El Camino Real), she came upon a peaceful knoll, where she lingered a while to admire the view and the beautiful surroundings. As mid-afternoon approached, she decided it was time to head back to her hillside house. Bidding goodbye to the knoll, she returned to the path and retraced her steps up the old Padre's Trail. She had gone only a short distance when she saw a strange gray cloud, "a sort of flowing fog," drifting down the path. As the fog came closer, it continued to follow the trail, appearing to be about as wide as two or three adults walking side by side. Suddenly the fog was upon her, but instead of enveloping her it parted and passed on each side. Frightened by what was happening, and bewildered about where the fog could have come from on such a clear and cloudless day, she moved to the side of the path and continued toward her house. Winding through the woods, the trail had a sloping bank and considerable foliage on one side, and a short drop and small gully on the other. Staying close to the bushes growing from the incline at the side of the trail, the woman watched as the fog passed by her and continued toward the mission. Anxious to understand what was taking place and feeling frightened of the strange fog, she became even more disconcerted as the movement of the fog created people-like shapes moving in a walking-like rhythm, almost as if the cloud were made up of human forms swaying to and fro as they sauntered down the trail. The fog even appeared to her to vary in height, as a small group of people would if they were walking one behind the other.

Clinging to the bushes as she went, the woman continued up the path until she reached a spot where the trail parted. At this junction she needed to cross the path and a small bridge on the other side. This also meant she had to break through the fog, which continued to flow down the trail. Not seeing an end to the mysterious cloud, the terrified woman summoned all her courage and beat her way through the fog with her fists, crying "Give way! Give way! Give way!" Upon making it safely to the other side, she dashed across the bridge and burst into the first house she came to (which, fortunately, was occupied by people she knew).

After calming their friend down and soothing her fears, her acquaintances listened in astonishment as she haltingly related her weird experience. Glancing at each other in awe, they checked a calendar, just to be sure . . . As they had suspected, it was a special day at the mission, a day on which padres from all over California visited Father Serra's historic church. As they explained the significance of the day to their friend, the people in the house suddenly heard the mission bells ringing in the distance—as if to welcome the faithful fathers who had followed the Padre's Trail to Carmel Mission to pay their respects.

## She was sighted on moonlit nights . . .

*June 27, 1980* According to a couple of elderly Pacific Grove residents,* around the turn of the century, a young woman was killed in the Palo Colorado Canyon of the Big Sur coast. They don't know how she lost her life, but they mentioned that when she was alive she was very attractive and had long, golden hair. For many years after her death her image was seen beside the creek that flows through the picturesque canyon. The sightings took place on moonlit nights, and when she was observed she was always combing her hair (the tellers of the tale surmised that she may have been using the light of the moon to see her reflection in one of the creek's pools). According to these Pacific Grove old-timers, the site where her image was seen was also the place she had been killed.

## The remains of up to forty people . . .

*September 13, 1980* A very old, and very knowledgeable, Monterey man stated that when Monterey was controlled by Spain (prior to 1822), the backyard of the old Whaling

---

* Now deceased.

60

Station was used as a burial place. Who was buried there is unknown—guesses have ranged from Indians to political prisoners—but according to his source the yard contains the remains of up to forty people!

Unfortunately, this account has several loopholes, the most obvious one being that the Whaling Station wasn't even built until the 1840s. If there is a germ of truth in the tale, however, it may help to explain some of the ghostly happenings that are said to take place within the building (some of which are discussed in "He was afraid to go into the room alone," page 46).

## His ghost scurries about the halls . . .

*September 13, 1980*   The late 1840s saw the construction of California's First Theater, which is still standing on the southwest corner of Pacific and Scott streets in Monterey. The structure was built by Jack Swan, an English seafarer (of Scottish ancestry) as a lodging house and barroom for sailors. However, it wasn't long before the building got its start as a theater. Several bored U.S. soldiers who were stationed nearby talked Swan into letting them use the facility as a makeshift theater. With the staging of the first play (listed as *Putnam, the Iron Son of '76*), the theater was born. This play is said to be the first dramatic performance in California to which an audience paid admission.

The building has served a variety of uses during its existence of almost 150 years, but since 1937 it has again been used as a theater. Evidently Jack Swan still keeps an eye on things—or so people familiar with "the house that Jack built" say. When things are not going as they should, his ghost can be seen scurrying about the halls and peering from the wings backstage.

Another sighting at the First Theater was reported by a security guard. The guard was crossing the street in front of the theater between 2:00 and 3:00 a.m. when he noticed a movement inside the bar section of the building. Knowing the structure was supposed to be empty, he crept up to a window and peeked in. To his surprise he saw an old man with a long white beard and stooped shoulders working about the bar as if he was familiar with the facility. Moving to a second window to get a better view, the guard lost sight of the man, and further checking turned up nothing. However, in discussing the incident later and telling about the man he had seen, the guard unknowingly described Jack Swan to perfection! This is all the more remarkable since, not being interested in local history, the security guard was unaware of the building's colorful past—and had never heard of Jack Swan.

As it turned out, the guard would soon be treated to another inexplicable apparition in the area of the First Theater. As with the first event, this incident occurred in the middle of the night. The guard had been relieved of his duties and, in the company of a second guard, was heading toward his car (which was parked in a multilevel garage across the street from the theater). Upon reaching the garage, the two men parted, as their automobiles were parked on different levels. Nearing his car, the first guard saw the shadowy but vaguely familiar figure of an elderly man hurry away from the area his vehicle was parked in and cross the street. The guard called for his companion, and the two of them crossed the street and looked around the theater grounds in a heavy fog. Not finding anyone or anything out of place, and wet from the fog, they soon tired of the search and returned to the garage. This time the second guard accompanied his partner to his car. When they reached the vehicle, they found a large, wet, white flower on the hood. Puzzled as to where the flower had come from, they decided to search the area around the parking garage. As might be expected, the only plant in the vicinity that had a flower similar to the one that was on the hood of the car . . . was in the First Theater's backyard!

# A wandering ghost or two . . .

*July, 1981* Not to be outdone by other publications, the June/July 1981 issue of *The Monterey Convention Guide* briefly discusses the Robert Louis Stevenson House. Other than indicating that it houses "the largest collection of Stevenson Memorabilia in the United States," the text also touches on the building's ghosts. Stating the structure is "said to have a wandering ghost or two," the article also suggests (perhaps with tongue in cheek) that the ghost of Stevenson himself has appeared in the room he occupied.

# The woman of his dreams . . .

*August 2, 1981* Taking place in a remote section of Monterey County, this account revolves around a man who was involved in a one-sided love affair. Although the woman of his dreams was a close friend, she did not feel the same fondness for him that he felt for her. Remaining a bachelor, the man lived his life longing for the lady he could not have. As the years passed, the woman became ill. Upon learning of her illness the man became greatly depressed. One day, feeling sad and alone, he took a walk in a nearby field. The day was dreary and heavy with fog, and as he walked he became lost in thought. Suddenly, hundreds of poppies scattered about the field opened as if it were a bright sunny day! Remaining open for only a few seconds, the poppies then closed again as if it were night. Not knowing the significance of this beautiful event, the man did not learn until later that the love of his life had passed away at the precise moment the poppies had opened.

## The sound of coffee being poured . . .

*August 11, 1981*  Today's brief notes each involve armory buildings in two Monterey Bay area communities. The first is said to involve a young National Guardsman who committed suicide in one of the buildings. For several years after this sad event, fellow Guardsmen told of hearing doors opening and closing at night, and of experiencing "a coldness" in the area where the tragedy took place.

The second series of events are thought to involve the ghost of a navy pilot. Even after moving from one armory facility to another, the ghost continued its haunting ways. As in the first account, manifestations included doors opening and closing, but in this instance the events took place both day and night. The ghost is also said to have created such a strong feeling of presence that dogs refused to venture into certain parts of the building. On one occasion five men who were in the armory's supply room spoke of hearing a door open, followed by the sound of coffee being poured. But when they investigated, there was no one there!

## A ball of fire bobbed in the water . . .

*August 19, 1981*  During the Second World War many of California's Japanese-Americans were placed in concentration camps. At one of these camps a Monterey man (who was approaching sixty) and a young man from Watsonville (in his late teens) became close friends. After the Japanese returned to their communities following the war's end, the two men again "planted their roots." As time went on the two friends lost contact with each other.

Then, in the late 1940s, the Watsonville man was leading a group of Boy Scouts on a Big Sur outing. While hiking along the Big Sur River, the scout leader saw a tear-shaped "ball of fire" bobbing in the water. (According to the man who recounted this tale, the Japanese have a word for such a thing, and the phenomenon usually is associated with death.) When he saw the fireball, the leader's thoughts turned to his wartime friend, and he had a tremendous desire to see him. Placing the scouts under the watchful eye of a second troop leader, he hurried to his car and raced to the home of his Monterey friend. Fearing the worst, the scout leader hesitatingly knocked on the door of the house . . . only to learn that his friend had died a few hours before.

Filled with grief at the news of his friend's passing, the scout leader thought again of the ball of fire. It was then that he realized his wartime buddy had died at about the time he had seen the fireball floating down the river!*

## Shadowy images in a bandit's hideout . . .

*September, 1981* Monterey's Vasquez Adobe is said to have been a hideout for California's notorious badman Tiburcio Vasquez (born in Monterey in 1835). The adobe was the home of his sister, and interestingly, it was—and still is—located behind the old Monterey jail (built in 1854).† Today the structure is owned by the City of Monterey and houses several city offices. Along with a handful of bandit tales, the adobe boasts a number of ghost stories, including happenings witnessed by several city employees. Among the incidents mentioned by these people are "swooshing" feelings, telephone lights that mysteriously blink, toilets that flush by themselves, the sounds of footsteps when no one is there, cold spots encountered in a downstairs room, and shadowy images.

---

* This account was told to me by the son of the man who died. It was he who had answered the door and broken the news of his father's death to the scout leader.

† The Vasquez Adobe is at 546 Dutra Street.

# A fat, grinning face appeared on the wall . . .

*September 24, 1981*   The lady who shared this account was raised in Pacific Grove. In reminiscing about the Eleventh Street house she lived in as a child, she mentioned several ghostly phenomena, including a curtain that raised and lowered by itself. This was witnessed by several members of the family, including a "very curious" German shepherd. Even more unnerving was a "fat, grinning face" that appeared on a bedroom wall! The three young people who saw the face were terrified. In their efforts to get out of the room, the lady said, they nearly "trampled each other."

In summing up her short series of tales, the lady said with feeling that she "hated the house!" In fact, she was so scared of the aged dwelling that on arriving home from school she would open the front door, throw in her books, and run!


# A gray-haired and affable ghost . . .

*October 17, 1981*   While at a book signing in Carmel Valley, I met a woman from San Diego who owned a Victorian house on Granite Street in Pacific Grove. Upon seeing my ghost books she began telling me about the ghost of an elderly lady who frequented the house. According to the tale (as it was told to her by the young daughter of a past tenant), the ghost visited the daughter's room on a once-a-week basis, and the two of them enjoyed several friendly conversations. The ghost lady was described as gray-haired, very pleasant, and dressed in old-fashioned clothes. In addition, the daughter reported, there was the mystery of the open drawers. It seems that several drawers were repeatedly found open when no one was in the house to open them. Perhaps, as has been suggested, the affable ghost was searching for something she had left behind.

## A woman's scream can be heard . . .

*October 21, 1981* Near Cannery Row is a large Victorian house. Thought to have been constructed by a ship captain, the building has been a Monterey landmark for many years. Among the many stories that circulate about the house is one of lost treasure. Exactly who hid the treasure and what it contained remain something of a mystery. As to ghosts, one account tells of a lady who was killed long ago in an upstairs room. The death took place at the height of a raging storm, and, the tale concludes, during fierce Pacific storms a woman's scream can sometimes be heard coming from an upstairs room!

## Ghosts of the days when the sardine was king . . .

*October 27, 1981* The word "ghost" means different things to different people. To some it means the sights, sounds, and smells of old that evoke memories and bring forth the ghosts of yesterday. Cannery Row abounds in such memories, particularly for those who knew the street when the sardine was king. Similar thoughts are expressed by JoAnne Hodgen Eaton in an article she wrote for the October 21, 1981, issue of *Coasting* (a Monterey Bay area newspaper and entertainment guide). In reference to Cannery Row, Ms. Eaton states, "The ghosts are there. They are in the decaying canneries, burned out warehouses and empty lots. They are heard rustling in the overgrown weeds along the Southern Pacific railroad tracks. They are the ghosts of cannery workers, bums and prostitutes who once inhabited a stretch of road that has become known as Steinbeck's Cannery Row." Perhaps only the old-timers know the true meaning of Ms. Eaton's prose, and it is for them that I record this note.

## Ghostly eyes stared at the family . . .

*October 28, 1981*   A local woman called today wondering whether I knew of someone who could rid her house of ghosts!

The woman indicated that four or five ghostly figures frequented the premises—perhaps a family, she suggested, since a man and woman, plus two or three children, have been observed. At least four people have experienced the ghostly happenings. She went on to say that among the happenings were "feelings of presence" and the sighting of ghostly eyes that stared at members of her family when they awoke in the middle of the night!

One additional occurrence adds a new dimension to the ghost stories I have recorded so far. According to the woman's husband, one night a ghost tried to tuck him in bed!

## The ghost follows him about the building . . .

*October 28, 1981*   In talking to a Cannery Row merchant I learned that the old Monterey Canning Company buildings* are said to harbor a ghost. Located in the heart of the Row's business district, the Monterey Canning Company buildings house numerous stores and restaurants. Several people are reported to have experienced the ghostly happenings, including at least one shopkeeper. However, the ghost has been most visible to the night watchman. It is he who claims that the ghost follows him about the buildings and even up the elevator.

* The buildings are on the corner of Cannery Row and Prescott Avenue.

## The presence had a smirk on its face . . .

*December 29, 1981* The village of Carmel-by-the-Sea has long been a gathering place for people of the arts. Sprinkled about the town are a number of dwellings that housed these people. Some of these buildings boast intriguing tales of the way it used to be, and some are said to boast ghostly figures that wander about.

One such structure, located near the beach, is a literary landmark of old Carmel. Not only did an internationally known author live there for many years, but rumor has it that fellow author John Steinbeck, as well as movie actor James Cagney, also lived there for short periods of time. Other literary links to the house include the visits of such acclaimed authors as Alice B. Toklas, Sinclair Lewis, Gertrude Stein, and Ernest Hemingway.

As to the building's ghost, a past worker at the house said that the image of a bearded, jolly (at times), flush-faced, heavyset man was often observed in the dwelling. The one (and only) time the worker entered the building through the front door, she saw the ghost sitting at a rolltop desk (which was messy and piled high with papers). On looking up from the desk, the presence had a smirk on its face. Even though the ghost is said to have usually been jolly, he was also known to have had a temper. On one occasion, the story goes, he became angry with someone who was talking about him. Grabbing the person by the wrist, he flipped her to the floor!

## Approximately twenty years after the poet's death . . .

*December 30, 1981* Legend has it that the great American poet Robinson Jeffers hinted he might haunt his Carmel Point home after his death. Knowing his affinity for the hawk (for which he named the striking stone tower he built next to his house), a handful of Carmelites wonder whether the spirit of the award-winning author might have returned to his beloved rock house this month, approximately twenty years after his death. It seems that on December 19 a hawk, rare on Carmel Point, was seen perched atop the roof of the rugged Jeffers home.

## She experienced a terrific pressure on her body . . .

*February 5, 1982*  Strange things are said to happen in and around a certain Carmel Valley home. (For more information on this Carmel Valley home, see "The bones of a long-dead Indian," page 102.) The events include unexplained accidents and tragic deaths. This information was related by the dwelling's owner, who reported that there was a haunted bedroom in the house. Visitors refuse to use the room, she said, and when she tried to sleep there, she experienced a "terrific pressure" on her body that prohibited her from getting out of bed. The bed is made of heavy metal, and upon occasion it has vibrated during the night, causing it to move up to six inches!

## She would never be able to stay in the house again . . .

*March 19, 1982*  I was talking with a popular Monterey Peninsula priest, and the conversation eventually got around to ghosts. It was then that he told me about a Pacific Grove house he had inherited many years before. At the time of the inheritance he and his wife did not live on the Peninsula. However, when possible, they would visit the area and stay in the structure, which was filled with furnishings that had belonged to the deceased former occupant. Unfortunately, when they stayed in the dwelling they were made very uncomfortable by the awareness of a "presence" that permeated the house. In an effort to make the building more livable (and perhaps to help diminish the feeling of presence), they rearranged the furniture upon each visit. However, when they returned to the structure at a later date, they would find the furnishings returned to their original positions. What made this all the more intriguing was the fact that they had the only key to the building.

On one occasion the priest and his wife loaned the house to a couple who were coming to the Peninsula for a visit. Upon returning the key, the wife stated she "would never be able to stay in the house again!" When asked why, she said that she awoke in the middle of the night to find the figure of a woman standing near the foot of the bed. The lady was matronly in appearance and was staring at her and her husband. The wife screamed and woke up her husband, whereupon the image disappeared. Of added interest to this tale is the word of the priest, who stated that neither he nor his wife had told the couple—or anyone else—about their ghostly experiences in the building.

## Spirits of another kind . . .

*April 3, 1982*  The Lara-Soto Adobe at 460 Pierce Street in Monterey was built in the 1840s. A century later, in 1944, it became the home of John Steinbeck. Among the books he is said to have worked on while living in the house was *The Pearl*.

Long before Steinbeck purchased the property, the building stood vacant and abandoned. It was during this period that the aged adobe became a hangout for drifters and thieves. "Spirits" of another kind were also said to frequent the premises, and several Montereyans believed the house was haunted. Interestingly, a book written for Monterey's Bicentennial Celebration (1970) states that the building was exorcised before it was lived in by Steinbeck.

## The house had a history of being haunted . . .

*April 5, 1982*   As I was enjoying a cup of coffee at a popular Carmel coffee shop, a fifty-year resident of the village invited me to join him at his table and began telling me about some ghostly happenings he and his wife had experienced. The house they lived in at the time was in the picturesque Carmel Point area. Among the events he described were light fixtures that swung back and forth when the day was still and void of breezes, floors that creaked when no one was walking on them, bathroom noises (including the sounds of running water), a dog that barked at unseen things, and a picture that fell forward when no one was near it. (The picture had been leaning against the mantel, and had been there for a long period of time.) The man said the house had a history of being haunted and that several people had moved from it because of the happenings.

When he and his wife decided to move to a second Carmel location, the man went on, they experienced strange happenings at their new residence as well. Among the odd occurrences was the distinct smell of wet ashes that woke them up each Sunday morning between the hours of 4:00 and 5:00 a.m. However, there was never any sign of fire or smoke, and the odor was only apparent at that time. Unfortunately, the man does not know the history of the house, and is unaware of any fires that may have taken place there.

## A spout of fire poured from its mouth . . .

*April, 1982*   According to an old article from the *Monterey Peninsula Herald*, Carmel poet Robinson Jeffers once told a tale about two Spanish cowboys who set out from Monterey on a trip to Big Sur. As they reached the top of Carmel Hill (between Monterey and Carmel), they heard the sound of a child crying in the nearby woods. Rushing to the spot, they found the baby . . . but as they picked it up, "a spout of fire poured from its mouth"! Needless to say, "they threw it away in horror" and hastily departed the scene. (A somewhat similar tale is recorded in "The rider was terrified to see fang-like teeth," page 51.)

## The ghostly image walked through the wall . . .

*June 11, 1982* I have learned some new details about the episode of the historian who saw the ghost of a Monterey priest in the front court of Carmel Mission (see "A long-dead priest," page 16). The information comes from an account he shared with one of his associates. According to this version, which was related to me after his death, the historian at first wondered whether someone had dressed up like his friend to try and scare or fool him. It was with this in mind that he decided to follow the figure to find out who or what it was. Upon nearing the church, the historian called out to the person. As the individual stopped and turned, the historian was shocked to see the face of his departed friend. He could only stare in awe as the ghostly image turned and continued on its way . . . walking through the wall of the church!

## The mystery of the burning candles . . .

*June 11, 1982* In discussing the circumstances surrounding the ghostly priest (see preceding note), I was also told the following tale. The setting for the story is Carmel Mission in the 1930s, when a new roof was being installed and other modifications were being made. During the restoration project a small substitute chapel was being used (where the museum library is now located). The incidents mentioned in this account took place in the substitute chapel.

The happenings occurred on Friday nights and involved six candles that were repeatedly burned to their base. This created something of a problem for the person who was in charge of the restoration project, and who also watched over the church, since he was required to make a trip to Monterey's Royal Presidio Chapel to get more candles. (According to the individual who told me this tale, at that time Carmel Mission was a branch of Monterey's Catholic church, and the Monterey church supplied the small chapel with candles and other necessities). Finally, after becoming fed up with the trips to Monterey, the project foreman asked the Carmel priest to be more careful and be sure the candles were out before he left the chapel. Surprised by this request, the priest insisted he always put the candles out, and when he did they were far from used up. Since both men were adamant about the candles, they were perplexed about what was taking place and agreed to check the candles together before locking the room that Friday night. Following this plan, on the appointed evening they inspected the candles. Finding them only partially burned, they locked the chapel door, even going to the trouble of putting a seal on it that would have to be broken before anyone could enter the room. Upon meeting the next morning, they checked the seal, found it intact, and entered the chapel. Heading straight for the candles, they were shocked to discover they were all burned to their base!

Vowing to find out what was going on, the priest and the foreman again sealed the door the following Friday night. This time, however, they hid in the courtyard, where they could keep an eye on the chapel window. Suddenly, in the middle of the night, they saw a faint glow through the colored glass. As they watched in wide-eyed wonder, the glow became brighter and brighter, indicating that more than one candle was being lit. Together they approached the chapel door, which was still affixed with the seal, and burst into the room. A quick inspection proved the room to be empty of people— and that all six candles were brightly burning!

In an attempt to understand the significance of this event, the priest and his companion discussed several stories that were circulating around the Peninsula at that time. These tales told of a local priest who had died and who supposedly had left a number of prayers unsaid. Perhaps, they reasoned, the spirit of this priest had returned to the mission to complete his prayers.

While this may seem a bit far-fetched, it is important to note there is more to the story than what can be related here. After so many years have passed, it is probably best to let the matter rest, as the baffling mystery of the burning candles comes no closer to being solved when the tales are told.

## They run from the room wearing only a towel . . .

*July 2, 1982*  A large old house on Pacific Avenue in Pacific Grove boasts a history of strange happenings. At one time the property was considered a showplace of the Grove, as its gardens were said to have been among the finest on the Peninsula. However, the structure sat vacant for several years, and as time passed the building and its grounds lost much of their "magic." According to a person who later lived in the house, the vacancy was explained by one of the original owner's last wishes, which stipulated that nothing was to be changed after her death. Unfortunately, with the building and grounds being neglected for such a long period of time, the house deteriorated and a jungle of sorts grew up around it. Today the structure has been converted to apartments and once again is occupied, but neither it nor its gardens have ever returned to their former glory.

A number of tales are told about odd occurrences connected with the property, several of them involving an aged chair. The chair is a red leather rocker and is thought to have belonged to the building's original owner. In fact, one source says the owner died while sitting in the chair. If this is true, it might help to explain why guests who used the chair did not stay seated for long. When asked why they suddenly rose from the rocker, the visitors invariably shrugged and mumbled something about an uncomfortable feeling that had come over them. Of added interest is information that indicates the chair has been offered for sale on numerous occasions, but when prospective buyers give it a try, they get strange looks on their faces and decide against it.

Other happenings at the house have taken place in the main bathroom. Among the most common of the occurrences are bodiless voices that are heard when someone is using the facility. People using the bathroom have become so frightened by the voices and the accompanying feelings of presence that they have exited the room on the run—wearing only a towel! According to another story, in a downstairs living room, a German beer glass "pushed itself" from a shelf and fell to the floor. The original position of the glass was such that it could not have fallen by itself. In addition, radios in the house stubbornly refuse to work properly for certain individuals—for example, repeatedly changing stations by themselves—even though they work quite well for others. Sounds of someone cooking emanate from the kitchen in the middle of the night when no one is there. In the outside garden area, on a windless day the trellis began to shake as if a great storm had descended upon it. No one could figure out what caused the shaking, but soon after it happened the trellis collapsed. All this may seem incredible, but most of the events related here have been witnessed by more than one person.


## The Lady in Lace of Pebble Beach . . .

*September 1, 1982*  Additional information has come to light regarding the Lady in Lace of Pebble Beach. As most local ghost enthusiasts know, the willowy figure of a lady dressed "in flowing robes of lacy white" has been seen in the vicinity of the Seventeen Mile Drive's famous Ghost Tree, near Pescadero Point.* Supposedly, several accidents have narrowly been avoided as motorists tried to avoid hitting the ghostly figure as she strolled down the center of the road on dark, foggy nights. Who the lady is, or whose ghost she represents, has never been satisfactorily answered. One theory that has recently been discussed suggests that the mysterious figure may be Dona Maria del Carmen Barreto. Dona Maria once owned much of the land that is now Pebble Beach. Desiring a house in the city, where "a woman could look out on life and romance," Dona Maria sold 4000-plus acres for $500 and purchased an adobe in Monterey, which was then California's capital. (The home Dona Maria purchased is still a part of old Monterey and can be seen at 615 Abrego Street.) These events took place in the early 1840s, and as time went on the land she sold became some of the most sought-after real estate on the California coast. Perhaps, the theory suggests, the ghost of Dona Maria remains in the area, regretting the pittance she received from the sale of this beautiful and valuable land—a meager 12 cents per acre.

## The feeling of presence mysteriously vanished . . .

*September, 1982*   John Steinbeck's boyhood home, at 132 Central Avenue in Salinas, is something of a shrine for Steinbeck enthusiasts. The grand old Victorian structure houses a popular restaurant on the main floor (operated by the Valley Guild, with proceeds going to local nonprofit organizations), and in the basement is a delightful shop

* The mysterious lady is mentioned briefly in my book *Ghosts, Bandits and Legends of Old Monterey.*

(also operated by the Valley Guild, and appropriately named Best Cellar). Other than the hundreds of visitors and workers who annually flock to the building, the house also boasts a ghost. Among the supernatural sightings that have been made is the silhouette of a man resembling Steinbeck himself. The figure has been seen by Valley Guild members who work in the restaurant and give tours of the building. The silhouette is most often observed in front of a window in the main downstairs front room.

Other happenings have also taken place in the house. One account tells of an incident that occurred before the facility was taken over by the Valley Guild. According to the person who told this tale, the structure was then operated as a dormitory for students attending Hartnell College, a nearby junior college. One summer when the house was almost empty of students, an individual who slept in what had been Steinbeck's bedroom told of being awakened in the middle of the night by the sounds of his door being opened and closed. As he glanced around the room to see who had come in, he found the room to be empty . . . except for a feeling of presence. The feeling was not scary and stayed in the room only a short time. Then, as if his invisible guest was satisfied with what it saw, the door again opened and closed, and the feeling of presence mysteriously vanished.

## The ghost of John Steinbeck . . .

*September, 1982* I chatted again with the woman who had shared the information about the Steinbeck house (see preceding note). She had once been a tour guide at the facility and was very knowledgeable about it. On this second meeting she showed me an article that had appeared in a "Great Ghost Stories" series of a newspaper (thought to be the *National Enquirer*). Even though the article was old and undated, it was of considerable interest because it discussed a ghostly figure that had been seen in Steinbeck's boyhood home. The sightings had been made by three people at different times, with none of the three knowing of the other sightings. In each sighting the image had been seen "in profile" and appeared to be centered in a "yellowish-white mist."

Of most interest to Steinbeck buffs, the figure resembled the Salinas-born author. When observed it seemed to be at ease and unaware of, or unconcerned about, the people around it. When it moved, it appeared to float or glide rather than walk.

These sightings were made in late 1971 and early 1972, approximately three years after Steinbeck's death. At this time part of the building served as a boarding house for Hartnell College students. The figure was seen both upstairs and downstairs. Evidently the house manager's dog also saw the apparition, since one night it began to bark fiercely at the ghostly image, and it was the dog's barking that resulted in the manager's original sighting.

## A hotel for ghosts . . .

*September 22, 1982*  While visiting a local print shop, I met a woman who told me about a medium who had visited an old Monterey building. The building, which had an interesting history of ghostly happenings, had been vacant for an extended period. While in a trance the medium communicated with several of the spirits that lived there. They, in turn, told her that when the building was empty it had served as a kind of hotel or temporary home for ghosts. Some of the ghosts didn't even know they were dead! When the medium explained the situation and told the spirits it was alright to "go on," many of them did just that!

# The Man in Gray . . .

*October, 1982*   There are many ghostly stories connected with old Monterey's Hotel Del Monte,* which is now the United States Naval Postgraduate School. A surprising number of them revolve around its mysterious Man in Gray.

The question of whose ghost the Man in Gray represents has never been satisfactorily answered, although numerous guesses have been made. Some have suggested that the Man in Gray (so called because of his gray hair, gray beard, and a gray suit he often wore) is the ghost of Charles Crocker, the famous rail baron who was one of California's Big Four. It was the Big Four (and their Pacific Improvement Company) that built the hotel, and the fabulous Del Monte was one of Crocker's pet projects. Rumor has it that a proud Charles Crocker was the first to sign the hotel's registration book at the grand opening festivities in 1880—and again in 1888, when the Del Monte reopened after a disastrous fire.

As to Crocker being the Man in Gray, it is of interest to note that bits of gray were "liberally" sprinkled about his hair and beard, which had once been fiery red, and it is not too much to assume that, on occasion, he wore a suit of gray. Without a doubt, however, the most convincing argument in favor of Crocker's spirit lingering about is that he died on August 14, 1888, in his Hotel Del Monte suite. Nevertheless, in fairness to Crocker, and to Del Monte ghost buffs, those who have seen the Man in Gray say that he is on the thin side, whereas Charles Crocker was big and burly (one source goes so far as to describe him as "glaringly overweight").

---

* As related in my book *Incredible Ghosts of Old Monterey's Hotel Del Monte.*

## No one in the building was in costume . . .

*October 22, 1982*   During a filming session for a television show at Monterey's Robert Louis Stevenson House, the building's guide told me of a recent incident there. One day a local woman (of more than middle age) was walking through the back garden area of the house. Having shopped at a nearby market, she was burdened with bags of groceries and decided to rest on one of the benches. After gaining a second wind, she gathered her groceries and continued on her way. (For those unfamiliar with the Stevenson House, there is a small park that leads from Munras Street to the Stevenson House gardens, and from there to Houston Street.) As she neared one of the building's rear windows, she paused and peeked inside. To her surprise, she saw a woman dressed in an old-fashioned Spanish costume sitting on an old wicker couch. When she reported her sighting to the guide, he could only inform her that no one in the building was in costume—and certainly no one should have been in the room, since it was off-limits to visitors!

## She was awakened by a slap in the face . . .

*October 31, 1982*   On Halloween day, as I was walking past a small Victorian house in the Cannery Row area, I was stopped by a fellow who lived there. After several kind comments about my books, he said there was a ghost in the house. With that he insisted I follow him into the building and meet the people who had experienced the happenings. I was introduced to a number of folks and listened to a variety of tales. Although all the stories were interesting, one account stands out in my mind. It seems that a young woman (she appeared to be in her twenties) was awakened one night by a slap in the face. The slap reminded her of the way her mother had slapped her when she was a child and had done something wrong. Upon looking around to see who had slapped her, she realized she was alone in the room. However, near the bed was a candle that had burned to its base and was in danger of starting a fire. Even though it wasn't her mother's ghost that had done the slapping— her mother was still alive—the thought was expressed that somebody (or something) was watching over her and that the slap was meant to rouse her from her sleep . . . and avoid a possible tragedy.

## Strange noises, chills, and poltergeist effects . . .

*December, 1982* While going through my notes preparing for a lecture, I came across the tape of a radio talk show I did in October of 1976. The show dealt with many of the subjects I had written about up to that time, such as shipwrecks, sea monsters, treasures, and ghosts. Included in the accounts that came from callers to the show were hints of strange happenings that had taken place in a gigantic old house perched high on a Santa Cruz hill. (The community of Santa Cruz borders the north shore of Monterey Bay.) Even more interesting to history buffs than the ghost stories was the caller's claim that the building's wiring was done by inventor Thomas Edison and that President Teddy Roosevelt once stayed there.

Monterey also shared in the callers' tales. One caller told about noises, chills, and poltergeist effects that had been experienced in the Royal Presidio Chapel's old rectory. As has previously been mentioned in these notes, this building is well known for its ghostly happenings, and the rumor that a priest had once been killed there (as commented on by the caller) only adds to its mystique. However, the key word for me is "rumor," since to date I have found no evidence indicating that a priest was ever killed in the rectory.

## Soon the house was considered haunted . . .

*December, 1982*   Many of Pacific Grove's picturesque Victorians are situated near the sea. The one discussed in this account boasts an attractive veranda with a walkway on top. Built in the 1880s, the house was originally used as a summer place for people wishing to escape the heat of California's Central Valley. Legend states that along the way a ship captain also occupied the building. Unfortunately, none of the Grove's old-timers I talked to knows who the captain was or when he lived there. However, several of the old-timers did vouch for the fact that the building sat vacant for several years. It was during this period that people began looking at the structure in peculiar ways, as odd occurrences were said to take place there. Soon the house was considered haunted, and stories of strange happenings were connected with it. Among the more interesting of the tales were accounts of a figure—looking like an old sea captain—who paced back and forth atop the veranda. Occasionally the figure would stop and look wistfully at the fog-shrouded sea. Fortunately for those who currently reside at the house, the building has been restored to its original splendor, and any ghostly guests have apparently departed the scene.

## The maid felt as if someone were checking up on her . . .

*January 19, 1983*   One of Pacific Grove's largest Victorians is located near the center of town. Built in the 1880s, the structure has served as a lodging house and hotel for approximately one hundred years. Today, after being totally restored, the facility is one of the Grove's most popular bed and breakfast inns. Over the years thousands of people have become a part of its history, so it is not surprising to learn that a spirit is said to lurk there. According to the manager of this landmark building, two maids have reported a presence in one of the suites. Of added interest is the fact that the maids reported feeling the same sensation, in the same suite, at different times, each unbeknownst to the other. In reporting the incidents to the manager, each maid indicated she felt as if she was not alone . . . almost as if someone were checking up on her to be sure things were being done right. For the record, the maids worked at the facility at different times and neither was aware of any supernatural happenings that had taken place within the structure.

## The men had disappeared . . .

*February 1, 1983* I received a letter today from a woman in California's Central Valley who had recently read my book *Ghostly Tales and Mysterious Happenings of Old Monterey.* She was excited about the work and wanted more information on local ghosts. Having been born and raised on the Monterey Peninsula, she also shared a few tales of her own. One story told about a girl who had been killed in Pacific Grove's Lovers Point area. A jealous lover was blamed for her death. On certain nights after the incident, people claimed to be able to hear the girl crying.

The letter writer also had a firsthand experience to share. The event took place when she was a teenager and was on Monterey's Del Monte beach with her boyfriend. It was late at night, and they were "hugging and kissing" when she looked up and saw three big men walking toward them. She told her boyfriend, but when he glanced in the direction she pointed, he couldn't see anyone. Even though they remained invisible to him, she continued to watch as the men got closer and closer. Finally, when they were only a short distance away, she exclaimed, "Let's get out of here!" Bewildered by what was taking place, her boyfriend was more than happy to vacate the scene. As she stumbled through the sand in an effort to get away, she turned to see whether her boyfriend was following . . . only to discover that the men had disappeared!

## The ghost of Herrmann Hall . . .

*March 14, 1983*  A little over a month ago (February 7) I learned of an incident that took place in the main corridor of the Naval Postgraduate School's Herrmann Hall.* The incident involved a woman who worked at the facility and who supposedly was pushed to the floor. The fall resulted in a broken wrist. This account concerned me, since I had heard several tales of ghostly happenings in the Herrmann Hall/Hotel Del Monte building, but none had ever mentioned anyone being hurt. Furthermore, the stories I had collected indicated that the ghost of Herrmann Hall—better known as the Man in Gray—was "friendly" and was not someone (or something) that would hurt people (see "The Man in Gray," page 80). With this in mind, I set out to find the person who had been pushed and hear her side of the story.

Today I succeeded in tracking this individual down. The information that follows is her (abbreviated) account. While walking down the main upstairs corridor of Herrmann Hall (near the chapel), she felt a slight movement—sort of a "swoosh"—by her side, as if someone was trying to get by. Surprised by the feeling, since she thought she was alone in the hall, she moved aside to let the person pass. While moving and glancing to her side—the corridor, incidentally, was empty—she lost her balance and fell. When I asked whether she thought she had been pushed, she emphatically said "No!" The fall, she said, was due to her own clumsiness. With this happy ending (except, of course, for the broken wrist), Postgraduate School personnel can rest assured that

---

* As previously mentioned, the Naval Postgraduate School was formerly the Hotel Del Monte. The structure now known as Herrmann Hall was the hotel's main building.

the Man in Gray (or whatever caused the "swoosh") didn't intentionally try to hurt anyone.

## The lady who haunts the lighthouse . . .

*March 23, 1983* One of the best-known buildings on the Monterey Peninsula isn't a mission, an adobe, or a Victorian (at least in the strict sense of the word). Instead, it is the Point Pinos Lighthouse, located near the southern tip of Monterey Bay. Having been in operation since 1855, this Pacific Grove landmark is the oldest continuously operating lighthouse on the Pacific Coast and has been designated a national historic site by the National Park Service. There are several interesting stories connected with the building and with those who served as "keepers of the light." Among these people was Charles Layton, the first person to be in charge of the facility. Unfortunately, Layton's career was cut short when he was killed in a shootout while serving as a member of a sheriff's posse.*

Another lighthouse keeper who is known to history buffs is Allen L. Luce. It was Luce who was visited, and written about, by Robert Louis Stevenson during Stevenson's brief stay in Monterey in 1879. As for female lightkeepers, Layton's widow, Charlotte, was in charge of the station in the late 1850s, and Emily A. Fish, also a widow, filled the post in 1893. A combined total of forty years of lighthouse-keeping service is represented by these two women. Mrs. Fish is perhaps the better remembered of the two, since she was known for a number of things, including her parties,

---

*In the shootout the notorious bandit Anastacio Garcia killed two other members of the posse and made good his escape. He was later captured and unceremoniously hung in his Monterey jail cell. (For more information about Garcia and his part in the bloody Sanchez treasure feud, see my book *Tales, Treasures and Pirates of Old Monterey*.)

her blooded horses, her French poodle (which proudly trotted alongside her carriage), and her high social standing in the community. Today, according to stories that circulate about the lighthouse, the spirit of Mrs. Fish is still much in evidence. Her presence has often been felt, several odd happenings are said to have taken place, and a variety of objects are known to have moved about, particularly those in upstairs bedrooms.

## She felt as if someone was in the house . . .

*April 10, 1983* Almost one year to the day after I talked to a man who told me about several strange happenings in his Carmel Point home (see "The house had a history of being haunted," page 72), I was able to visit with the woman who currently lives there. After I explained who I was and why I was interested in the building, she informed me that she was happy with the house. However, she went on to say that this had not always been the case. When she originally moved into the building, she shared it with a friend. It was then that she was uncomfortable. Not only was she bothered by nightmares, but she frequently felt as if someone was in the house who shouldn't be there. What caused her to feel differently after her friend left is something of a mystery, since there was no ill will between them and they parted on good terms. Perhaps there were spirits within the building that for unknown reasons didn't want her friend to be in the house and made it uncomfortable for all until she moved out. Whatever the case, the current resident is now quite content, and even though there are moans, groans, creaks, and the sound of an occasional raccoon lumbering across the roof, she plans to stay put and enjoy the ambiance of her Carmel cottage by the sea.

# A ghostly figure passed him in the hall . . .

*April 10, 1983*  While in the Cannery Row area of Monterey, I chatted with a woman whose husband was stationed at the Naval Postgraduate School in the 1950s. In talking about the colorful history of this facility (including its ghosts and the activities that took place there when it was the Hotel Del Monte), she told me about an experience a naval officer had there in 1951. According to her account, early one morning (around 3:00 a.m.) the officer entered the main building, only to have a ghostly figure pass him in the hall! The image was very real and was that of a man "dressed in clothes of long ago." Upon telling others about his sighting, the officer received much good-natured teasing. Some suggested he had been drinking too much, while others joked about his seeing things that weren't there. In spite of the comments, the officer stuck to his story and swore he had seen the ghost of Herrmann Hall.

Built in the 1830s, the Robert Louis Stevenson House was known as the French Hotel when the little-known Scotsman stayed there in 1879. (Photo by L. Blaisdell)

Ghostly trees point to the back of Monterey's Robert Louis Stevenson House. (Photo by L. Blaisdell)

The nursery of the Robert Louis Stevenson House has been the scene of several ghostly happenings. (Photo by L. Blaisdell)

Before Monterey's Hotel Del Monte was destroyed by fire (in 1887, and again in 1924), it was known as "The Most Elegant Seaside Establishment in the World" and "The Queen of American Watering Places." (Photo by C. W. J. Johnson, courtesy U.S. Naval Postgraduate School Museum)

The front desk and a portion of the Hotel Del Monte's lobby as it appeared before fire destroyed its Victorian splendor. Also shown are the ghostly images of several of the hotel's guests. Although a photographer might explain how this effect was achieved, it is of interest to note that on the back of the aged photo someone once wrote, "Hotel lobby with 'ghosts.'" (Photographer unknown, R. A. Reinstedt collection)

The Monterey County Symphony plays its annual "Concert in the Park" on the grounds of the United States Naval Postgraduate School (formerly the Hotel Del Monte), home of the mysterious Man in Gray. (Photo by John Haley Scott, courtesy U.S. Naval Postgraduate School)

Dedicated in 1795, the Royal Presidio Chapel (left foreground) continues to serve as Monterey's main Catholic church. The chapel's old rectory (right) is of more recent vintage. Together they boast several ghost stories. (Photo by R. A. Reinstedt)

Built in the 1830s, the Stokes Adobe was the home of Gallatin's, a popular Monterey restaurant, during the 1950s, 60s, and 70s. During this period several ghostly happenings took place there. (Photo by L. Blaisdell)

93

California's First Theater is known for more than its melodramas. It was in the bar section of the building (inset) that the ghost of Jack Swan is said to have been seen. (Photos by L. Blaisdell)

Monterey's old Whaling Station was the headquarters of Monterey Bay's Old Company of Portuguese whalers in the 1850s. More recently, the attraction of its whalebone sidewalk, beautiful garden, and wonderful restoration has been embellished by tales of ghostly happenings. (Photo by L. Blaisdell)

Prize-winning author John Steinbeck lived and worked at Monterey's Lara-Soto Adobe in the 1940s. Abandoned for many years before Steinbeck owned it, the aged adobe was thought to be haunted by several early Montereyans. (Photo by R. A. Reinstedt)

Bandit tales and ghost stories are told about the Vasquez Adobe, once home to the sister of California's famed badman Tiburcio Vasquez. Currently owned by the City of Monterey, the building continues to be the site of ghostly occurrences. (Photo by L. Blaisdell)

Old-timers say that Cannery Row boasts a variety of ghosts, including a mysterious presence who frequents the old Monterey Canning Company buildings. (Photo by R. A. Reinstedt)

John Steinbeck helped to make Cannery Row famous, but today it's the Monterey Bay Aquarium that keeps the Row in the news. Certainly lesser known than the facility's magnificent exhibits are stories of ghosts that visit the premises. (Photo by R. A. Reinstedt)

In operation since 1855, Pacific Grove's Point Pinos lighthouse is the oldest continuously operating lighthouse on the Pacific Coast. Several strange happenings are rumored to have taken place there. (Photographer unknown, courtesy Pacific Grove Heritage Society)

Pacific Grove's Victorians come in all shapes and sizes . . . as do the ghosts that sometimes visit them. (Photo by C. W. J. Johnson, courtesy Pacific Grove Heritage Society)

Standing alongside the scenic 17 Mile Drive in Pebble Beach is the fabled Ghost Tree. It is in this area (near Pescadero Point) that the mysterious Lady in Lace has most often been seen. (Photographer unknown, R. A. Reinstedt collection)

Founded in 1770, lovely Carmel Mission was the hub of California's coastal mission chain. It was in the mission's front court that the ghostly figure of a "long-dead priest" was seen. (Photo by L. Blaisdell)

Situated along Monterey County's rugged Big Sur coast, Point Sur was a landmark to seafarers even before a lighthouse was built there in 1889. Also constructed were facilities for "keepers of the light." The inset shows the largest of these structures. Ghostly sounds of a woman coughing are reported to have been heard in a third-floor bedroom of this building. (Photos by L. Blaisdell and R. A. Reinstedt [inset])

# The sound of heartbeats came from her bed . . .

*May 20, 1983* Over a cup of coffee in Carmel I again talked to the man who had told me about several odd occurrences that had taken place in his Carmel Point home (see "The house had a history of being haunted," page 72). When I mentioned that I had visited the lady who currently lives there (see "She felt as if someone was in the house," page 87), he seemed pleased and returned to the subject we had previously discussed. Among the new accounts he had to offer was one which I found of particular interest.

The incident involved his eight-year-old daughter, who was having trouble sleeping. Two to three times a week she called him into her bedroom and complained of thumping sounds (similar to heartbeats) coming from her bed. Although he couldn't hear the sounds (even when he lay on the bed), his curiosity got the best of him, and he began checking into the history of the house.

It was then that he learned it was one of the first buildings in the area and had been lived in for many years by two elderly ladies. One of the ladies was said to have been a doctor and was thought to have died in the house. This he found to be of extreme interest, since the building had been furnished when they moved in, and, in all probability, the furniture they used had belonged to the ladies. With this in mind he wondered whether his daughter was sleeping in the same bed the lady had died in. If so, might there be a connection between the heartbeat sounds his daughter heard and the lady's death? Unable to find answers to such questions, he finally decided to let the matter drop. However, in adding a bit more substance to the tales he had previously told, he mentioned a well-known local artist who had once occupied the dwelling and who also reported odd occurrences in the house.

101

## The bones of a long-dead Indian . . .

*June 7, 1983*  Not far from Carmel is a house that boasts a ghostly presence. The presence (or force) has been felt by a number of people and apparently been a part of the structure since it was built in the 1950s. Even though most of the people who are familiar with the force describe it as being more annoying than hostile, at least one person disagrees. In telling about her experiences in the building, the owner of this large and well-built house describes such things as sucking sounds coming from the main bedroom and a force or presence that pounces on her in the middle of the night and pins her to the bed (as related in "She experienced a terrific pressure on her body," page 70). Not only does the invisible presence hold her down, but it makes it impossible for her to move her hands and arms. She has also experienced vibrations in the large metal bed, causing it to move on its own. Cold spots have also been felt in the house— most noticeably in the main bedroom, the hallway leading to the bedroom, and the dining area. Because the cold spots appear to move when people approach them, various individuals have suggested the presence may be uncomfortable around people and does its best to avoid them. Also, research indicates that several strange and tragic accidents have taken place across the street from the house. This information causes the owner of the building considerable concern and makes her wonder whether it is the land that is haunted rather than the house. The fact that the bones of a long-dead Indian were found on the property doesn't help her to rest any easier!

## The dark watchers of the Santa Lucias . . .

*June 9, 1983*  Fifty years ago today an article appeared on the front page of the *Monterey Peninsula Herald*. The title read "Mystery Woman Hermit Is Reported Living Below Big

Sur." While she was neither ghostly nor otherwise supernatural, the article was interesting. The lady hermit was
said to subsist "in true frontier fashion," killing game for
food, raising a few chickens, and felling trees for firewood.
Even though her identity remained a mystery, there was
speculation that she was the woman the famed Carmel poet
George Sterling addressed several of his poems to. Supposedly, this woman was a former Carmel resident who had
disappeared "under strange circumstances." The article
indicated that this early Carmelite was thought to be "living in seclusion" in the coastal mountains.

I can't help but wonder whether there is a connection
between the hermit woman and the famed "dark watchers"
of the Santa Lucias. (Robinson Jeffers and John Steinbeck
buffs are familiar with the "watchers" through Jeffers'
poem "Such Counsels You Gave to Me" and Steinbeck's
short story "Flight.") These works were published in the
1930s, the very time when the "mystery woman" was adding her own mystique to Monterey County's rugged coastal
peaks.

## The dish flew to the center of the room . . .

*June 21, 1983*  As I was chatting with a prominent Monterey man, he began telling me about a ghostly experience
he had had while living in Pacific Grove. The episode took
place in the kitchen of a small Victorian on 10th Street
when only he and his brother were in the room. As they
were facing each other, engrossed in conversation, a small
butter dish suddenly took off from the top of the refrigerator
(which was against the wall and in view of both of them) and
flew to the center of the room. Here it fell to the floor and
broke. Staring in astonishment at the broken pieces, the
men were at a loss to explain what had happened. The Monterey man added that cold spots were also felt in the house
and that a death had once taken place there.

## She screamed at the ghost to stop ...

*July 12, 1983*   This account comes from a man who once lived with his grandmother on 13th Street in Pacific Grove. This was perhaps as many as forty years ago, and the house has long since disappeared (it is thought to have been destroyed by fire). In reminiscing about the house, the man said his grandmother told him about several ghostly happenings that took place there. Among the things she blamed on the ghost were pictures that fell from the wall, chandeliers that were found on the floor, and glasses that shattered while they were on the dinner table. Ultimately his grandmother became so frustrated with what was taking place that she ran into the yard and screamed at the ghost, telling it to stop what it was doing or she would burn the house down! Apparently her outburst worked, since the ghostly happenings abruptly stopped! (Hmm ... If the house *was* destroyed by fire, and if his grandmother *had* threatened to burn the building down if the ghostly happenings didn't stop ... could it be that the ghost later returned, prompting her to follow through with her threat?)

## The original furniture was still in use ...

*July 26, 1983*   After many tries I was able to talk to the current owners of the haunted Carmel Point house (see "The house had a history of being haunted," page 72, "She felt as if someone was in the house," page 87, and "The sound of heartbeats came from her bed," page 101). After I had shared with them several stories of strange happenings that were said to have taken place there—including information about the two ladies who had lived in the structure for so many years—the owners indicated that the ladies had lived there, and that one of them was a relative of theirs. They denied, however, that either woman had died in the house. They also explained that neither of the women had been a doctor, though both had been nurses in the First World War. As to ghostly happenings in the house, the owners hadn't experienced anything out of the ordinary (though it should be noted that they did not themselves use the building as a residence).

As our conversation continued, they went on to say that one of the women who had lived in the house for more than thirty years had eventually become bedridden. It was during this time that she became quite "strange." Among her peculiarities was her insistence that the window shades be down at all times. She also had a rule against visitors and would not allow any "outsiders" in the house. The original furniture, they added casually, was still in use.

This last comment led me to wonder once again whether the bed in which the eight-year-old girl had heard the heartbeats was the same bed the bedridden nurse had slept in (see "The sound of heartbeats came from her bed," page 101). If so, could the heartbeats be those of this "strange" woman who had obviously spent many trying years in the structure?

## The night manager began keeping a log . . .

*August 2, 1983* After teaching a class about the fascinating history of old Monterey at the Naval Postgraduate School, I met with the building's night manager. During our conversation he indicated he had followed my advice and was keeping a log of the ghostly activities that took place in Herrmann Hall, once the main building of the Hotel Del Monte. Among the incidents he had recently recorded were the following:

1. Chairs had disappeared while he was in the downstairs dining room talking to a small group of people who had inquired about the Man in Gray (see "The Man in Gray," page 80). Several of the people were witnesses to the disappearance of the chairs, and all were at a loss to explain where they went.

2. Sounds of things moving (such as crates, dishes, and pots and pans) were heard in the kitchen at a time when it was empty of people and securely locked. Upon being checked the kitchen appeared to be in order, and there was no one to be seen. The sounds of faucets being turned on and off were also heard when the kitchen was empty.

3. The faucets in the main downstairs men's room also turned on by themselves (or perhaps at the command of a ghostly hand). A female member of the Quarterdeck's graveyard shift was walking along the downstairs hall around 4:00 a.m. when she heard the faucets in the men's room being turned on. (The Quarterdeck area of Herrmann Hall is near the main entrance and formerly housed the hotel's registration desk.) Not aware of anyone wandering about the halls at that time, she opened the door and called in. Upon receiving no reply, she stepped into the room to see all four faucets going full blast . . . though no one was in the room. She also reported an "icy" feeling in the area.

4. While working at his desk a fellow administrator reported that the lights in his office suddenly blinked off. Being alone in the room, he immediately glanced at the light switch and saw that it was moving by itself!

5. After losing his keys and turning his office upside down in an attempt to find them, the night manager discovered them locked securely in his safe . . . even though he was the only one on duty who knew the combination.

## The mysterious disappearance of clothes . . .

*August 19, 1983*   As I was chatting with an administrator from the City of Pacific Grove, he mentioned how much he enjoyed my books and that he thought one of the buildings I had written about was a house he currently lived in (a Victorian on 16th Street). In addition to the handful of happenings I had already described, he said one of the things that continued to bother him was the mysterious disappearance of clothes that had been hung on the backs of chairs.

## His face was gaunt and gray . . .

*September 13, 1983*   After one of my history classes at the Naval Postgraduate School, I was introduced to one of the bartenders at Herrmann Hall's popular Trident Bar. She proceeded to tell me about an experience she had had with the Man in Gray in the service elevator (see "The Man in Gray," page 80). As her story goes, one evening while she was helping to set up for a function in the ballroom, she needed some things she thought were downstairs. Taking the service elevator to the lower level, she began looking for the items. Unable to find what she was looking for, she returned to the empty elevator, pulled the hand-operated gate and door shut, pushed the button, and began her ascent to the second floor. As she faced the door, she began to feel a presence in the elevator and heard breathing sounds behind her. Spinning around, she saw the lifelike— "but almost dead appearing"—figure of a man! His eyes were sunken, and his face was gaunt and gray. His hair and beard were also gray. Standing very still, he leaned against the back of the elevator, with his hands hanging down in front of him. He wore an old-fashioned gray suit with an odd-appearing jacket that came to his waist. He also wore a vest, complete with a chain that attached to his pants. The suit looked old and "grungy." The man did not speak, or make any movements toward her, as she cowered against the door and stared at him.

"After what seemed like ages," the elevator finally reached the second floor. When it came to a stop, she frantically threw open the door and gate, and practically fell out! Anxiously she told the first person she came to about her frightening experience, but the individual ridiculed her and "pooh-poohed" her story. As a result she rarely discusses the sighting, except with people who won't put her down and who are sincerely interested in the Hotel Del Monte's Man in Gray.

## He saw a "faceless" figure staring at him . . .

*September 13, 1983*   Also in the Postgraduate School's Trident Bar (see preceding note), a local policeman and fellow history buff told me about a strange experience he had had in the Santa Lucias. The happening occurred in 1975, while he was hunting rabbits along Monterey County's south coast. As he was hiking in a remote area, he saw what appeared to be a "faceless" figure staring at him uncannily through "eyeless sockets." The stare was so intense it seemed to pass right through him and "peer off into the distance." Much of the figure's face was covered, "as if by a bandanna." Its body was cloaked in a black cape or poncho, with a hat or hood covering most of its head. Between the time the policeman glanced down at his rifle to cock it and looked up again, the figure vanished! With a sighting such as this having been made by a respected local citizen, I can't help but wonder whether the policeman had seen one of the Santa Lucias' mysterious dark watchers (mentioned in "The dark watchers of the Santa Lucias," page 102).

## Many bad things had happened there . . .

*September 20, 1983*   After teaching my history class at the Naval Postgraduate School, I met once again with the night manager of the facility. During our conversation he told me a strange tale about the woods behind the Monterey Presidio. (The Monterey Presidio dates back to 1770 and has played a colorful part in California history. Its original location was a short distance—less than a mile—from its present site. Today it is one of two presidios left in the state and is the home of the U.S. Army's Defense Language Institute.) As stated by the night manager, an acquaintance of his told him about two army officers, a man and a woman, who were hiking in the pine forest behind the current presidio. Suddenly they came upon an individual who was dressed like a conquistador—complete with helmet and breastplate! Upon conversing with him (whether in Spanish or English, I do not know), they were told that he had been killed long ago in a dispute over money or valuables of some other kind. Questioned further, the conquistador stated that the man who killed him had only wounded him at first and had thrown his body into the underbrush. Later the man returned and made sure he was dead. The two soldiers should leave the area, the figure added, because it was evil and many bad things had happened there.

## Candles were lit at the ghost's favorite table . . .

*September 20, 1983*  After the night manager at the Naval Postgraduate School told me about the conquistador sighting (see preceding note), he introduced me to an older woman who had played on the Hotel Del Monte grounds as a child and later worked at the facility as an adult. My new acquaintance reminisced a while about her childhood and how delightful it had been to stroll about the grounds and get lost in the hotel's maze (which was made of carefully cropped hedges and stretched to an amazing half-mile in length). She then talked about her days as a clerk in the hotel's elegant I. Magnin store, one of several quality retail outlets located in the hotel's main building. Among the guests she remembered seeing were Ava Gardner and Mickey Rooney (when they honeymooned at the hotel), and Errol Flynn ("who flirted with all the ladies").

The woman then brought up the subject of ghosts, saying that the only experience she had ever had with the Man in Gray occurred later in her career, when she worked as a waitress at the Postgraduate School (see "The Man in Gray," page 80). On two occasions, several weeks apart, when she and a second waitress were in the main downstairs dining room, they found candles mysteriously lit at the ghost's "favorite table." This account is of special interest because in interviewing other Postgraduate School employees for my book *Incredible Ghosts of Old Monterey's Hotel Del Monte*, I learned that candles were found burning in dining areas throughout the facility, including the ballroom, the La Novia Room, and the main downstairs dining room. Incidentally, when live music was played in the main dining room, it was said, the Man in Gray's "favorite table" was directly to the left of the bandstand.

## Four-footed ghosts . . .

*October 21, 1983* While enjoying my afternoon cup of coffee, I was joined by a Carmel man who had been born and raised in the community. In the course of our conversation the subject of cats came up. This led to the discussion of a Carmel house that is said to have cat ghosts prowling about. Not only do these four-footed ghosts climb up on beds and nap (the indentation of their bodies is said to be quite evident), but one huge cat (estimated to weigh as much as twenty pounds) was described as having a very "uncat-like" personality. This cat, it was suggested, is the reincarnation of an individual who once lived in the house.

## The spirit is considered nice . . .

*October 21, 1983* A City of Monterey administrator told me about several strange things that were taking place at the Vasquez Adobe, some of which I have already recorded (see "Shadowy images in a bandit's hideout," page 65). The current happenings, she indicated, didn't appear to be related to the famed California badman Tiburcio Vasquez. As described by the city administrator, the goings-on at the adobe, which now houses several city offices, include the following:

1. When only one person is in the building, a phone light will go on, indicating that someone else is using one of the telephones . . . but no one is ever there.

2. A person working alone in the downstairs section (where the only outside steps leading to the second floor can be seen) will suddenly hear footsteps overhead, even though no one else is in the building. Workers have also heard the stairs creak, as if someone were climbing them, though a quick check revealed nothing. In addition, the upstairs toilet has a habit of flushing when no one is on the second floor.

3. On several occasions things have inexplicably disappeared from various parts of the building.

4. Also on several occasions, people have experienced a "feeling of presence" and have had the sensation of someone (or something) passing them, as if the presence was moving from one room to another.

The city administrator added that among those who have experienced the happenings, the spirit or presence is considered "nice" and that it hasn't caused anything too "eerie or spooky" to take place.


## Could it be . . .

*October 21, 1983*  Could it be that the ghost of Father Junipero Serra returns to Carmel Mission each New Year's night? Reportedly his ghost has frequently been seen there during the New Year's night mass.

## To this day they wonder who played the trumpet...

*October, 1983*  Several years ago a Catholic high school was located next to Monterey's Royal Presidio Chapel and its old rectory. At the time this story took place, the school was active in local athletic contests and boasted a spirited group of cheerleaders and songleaders. Against the wishes (and rules) of the nuns who ran the school, this group of girls decided to explore the upstairs section of the old rectory to see what they could see and find out why it was off-limits to students. After sneaking up the stairs during a lunch recess, they quietly explored the different rooms. In the process they discovered several musical instruments packed in boxes. Thinking the instruments could be used for pep rallies, the girls excitedly sorted through the boxes looking for a trumpet. After opening all the boxes and finding nothing resembling a trumpet, the girls were shocked to hear the unmistakable sounds of just such an instrument coming from an adjoining room! Not waiting to see who the talented trumpet player was, the girls left the room on the run. Because of the commotion they caused, they were caught by a nun and severely reprimanded. To this day they wonder who played the trumpet . . . and to this day—more than a quarter of a century after the event—the lady who told me the tale (who happened to be a member of the group) refuses to go into the upstairs section of the old rectory.

## All the crystals tinkled in unison...

*November, 1983*  While skimming through an aged Monterey newspaper, I came across an article about local ghosts. Some of the stories I was familiar with (and had recorded in my books); others were new to me, and I found them to be quite interesting. One such tale took place at the Stokes Adobe in the heart of Monterey. Built in the 1830s, the Stokes Adobe was considered one of the most lavish homes in the area and was described as a social center of old Monterey. The adobe hosted many of Monterey's early Cascarone Balls, a festive gathering and dance that is held to this day. More recently, the attractive two-story structure served for many years as a popular and prize-winning restaurant. (Incidentally, to the rear of the adobe are the remains of the first kiln in the state.)

It was during its early years as a restaurant, in the 1950s, that this event took place. Late one night, after attending a social function, the restaurant owner and his wife stopped by the structure for a nightcap. The restaurant having already closed for the evening, they let themselves in and shared a glass of champagne. Upon hearing noises coming from the upstairs, the wife decided to investigate. As she climbed to the top of the stairs, she heard women's voices engaged in the kind of chatter one might expect to hear at an early Monterey party. Standing at the doorway of the room from which the voices came, the wife called into the room in Spanish, telling the ladies they were welcome to stay, as long as they turned the place back to its owners in the morning. Upon returning to her husband, she told him what had taken place, only to have him scoff at her and tell her she was "nuts." However, as they prepared to leave, the wife again called out to the ladies (singling out an individual she referred to as Carmencita) and said, "If you're there and can hear me, please give us a sign." With that, the story goes, "all of the crystals in every one of the chandeliers tinkled in unison"! Needless to say, from that time on both the owner and his wife were believers in ghosts!*

---

* For more ghostly happenings at the Stokes Adobe, see my book *Ghostly Tales and Mysterious Happenings of Old Monterey*.

## The cat went crazy . . .

*January 18, 1984* One of Monterey's most beautiful adobes is said to boast a presence in its upstairs back bedroom. Experienced by people over a period of many years, the presence is strong enough to keep the maid from cleaning the room—or at least to make it uncomfortable for her when she is there. But perhaps it is the reaction of the housekeeper's cat that best demonstrates the fact that something strange is associated with the room. When the cat was first introduced to the building, it "wanted to go exploring." Upon venturing into the back bedroom it "went crazy and couldn't be controlled!" The back bedroom is the only part of the house that caused the cat to react in such a way, and it has not wanted anything to do with the room since. No one seems to know who or what haunts the bedroom, but the presence only adds to the mystique of this "Queen of Monterey's Adobes."

## The ghost of Charlie Chaplin . . .

*January 20, 1984* An administrator at the Naval Postgraduate School and I sat in his Herrmann Hall office and talked about ghosts. The administrator (a naval officer) shared several incidents with me, a few of which I'll record here.

1. A woman was working alone one weekend in the upstairs dental wing. After completing her duties, she prepared to leave. As she was walking down the hall, passing several offices on the way, she heard a door close behind her. Knowing she was alone in the facility, and knowing of several strange happenings that had taken place within the clinic (including a number of sightings of the Man in Gray), she quickened her pace and exited the area as fast as she could!

114

2. In the same general vicinity, a dental technician told of being alone in the lab late one night. While hard at work preparing plates for the following day, he heard the main door of the dental clinic close, followed by the sounds of footsteps coming down the hall. As the footsteps drew near, sounding as if they were just outside the lab, the technician looked up to see who was there. To his amazement a gray cloud was all that he could see. His immediate reaction was that the pipe to the lab's old-fashioned steam heater had broken, creating the cloud. As he jumped up to investigate, the cloud vanished . . . and he could find no broken heater pipes to account for it. So shaken was the technician that he gathered his things and rushed from the room. To this day he refuses to work alone at night in the lab.

3. A woman living in one of the "cottages"* on the Post-graduate School grounds was working around the house when she saw the ghostly image of a man who looked like Charlie Chaplin. More concerned than scared, the woman mentioned the sighting to her husband when he got home from work. In discussing the incident, the couple wondered whether Chaplin had ever stayed in the cottage. (During the Del Monte's heyday it catered to many of Hollywood's famous personalities, and Chaplin is known to have visited the hotel on several occasions.) With the mystery unsolved, the couple decided not to tell their teenage daughter about the sighting.

A few days later, however, the daughter also reported seeing the ghostly image of a man. Her description matched that of her mother—and filmdom's famous comedian and pantomimist Charlie Chaplin!

---

*When the Postgraduate School was the Hotel Del Monte, several of the outbuildings were referred to as cottages, even though they were larger than many homes. They were usually occupied by guests who desired more spaciousness and seclusion than the hotel rooms offered.

Incidentally, while the administrator and I were discussing the many strange happenings that had taken place at the facility, the men's room toilet directly across the hall from his office flushed repeatedly, even though no one was in the room. When I asked about this, the officer smiled and said not to worry. "It happens all the time!"

## The Man in Gray pleaded for her help . . .

*February 24, 1984*  Around nine o'clock this evening I became involved in a fascinating ghostly happening. It began with a phone call from the night manager of the Naval Postgraduate School's dining room facility. He excitedly told me about an elderly lady who was in attendance and who was "in touch" with the Man in Gray (see "The Man in Gray," page 80). The manager said she would be willing to talk to me if I could hurry on down.

Grabbing my tape recorder, I jumped into my car and made a beeline for the Postgraduate School. Upon meeting the lady and her husband (a retired navy officer), I learned that they were celebrating their wedding anniversary. Unfortunately, their anniversary dinner hadn't turned out as they had planned. Because of the woman's frailty, her husband had left her off at the entrance to the building's west wing as he parked the car some distance away. While making her way toward the dining room, the wife felt a cool breeze on her neck and then saw the ghostly image of a man! As she quickened her pace in an effort to get away from the apparition, the phantom-like figure started talking to her and requesting her help. The farther she went, the more insistent he became. Finally, he began pleading with her to help him "find the stairs" and the woman who was atop them calling out to him. Seeing both the stairs and the woman, but being afraid of the ghostly presence, the lady hurried from the hall as fast as she could. Upon meeting her husband at the entrance to the dining room, she told him

116

what had happened. Realizing that his wife was both frightened and concerned, her husband tried to soothe her fears and get her mind off the subject by suggesting they go to their table and begin dinner.

It was then that the night manager became involved. Seeing the lady sitting at her table, obviously upset and unable to eat, he inquired about the food and asked whether there was anything he could do. Indicating that the food was fine, the wife explained about her disconcerting experience. She even said she could still see the man through the dining room doorway, standing in the hall and crying. Upon hearing her story, the night manager told her about my interest in the Hotel Del Monte's ghosts and asked whether she would be willing to share her experiences with me. After a short pause, the lady agreed to talk to me if I could get there before they left.

Upon my arrival introductions were made, and the lady, the night manager, and I walked to the spot where she had first encountered the presence. We were joined later by her husband, who remained in the dining room to pay the bill, and the night manager's brother, who had also been contacted. (While working at the Postgraduate School several years before, the brother had had a number of Man in Gray encounters.) Fetching the lady a chair, we made her as comfortable as possible. After getting her permission and promising to honor her wish to remain anonymous, I turned on my tape recorder and we began to talk.

As the woman started to tell me about her experiences, the ghostly presence suddenly reappeared to her. Even though I could not see anything, it was obvious that someone—or something—had materialized and made itself known to her. It was about this time that the night manager's brother arrived. He, too, could see the presence, and he indicated it was definitely the Man in Gray (the same ghostly figure he had seen on previous occasions). As the tape recorder ran, the Man in Gray continued to plead for the lady's help. She again became very upset, both because she felt sorry for the man and because she was unable to help him. Finally, she became so emotional, and the experience became so exhausting to her, that she said she couldn't "take any more." I turned off the tape recorder, and with the help of her husband she got up from the chair. After good-nights were said, they slowly made their way out of the building. As the night manager, his brother, and I remained in the hall, talking about what had taken place, the lady's husband returned to say that his wife wanted us to know she "doesn't drink" and that whatever it was she had experienced had not been brought on by alcohol.

What to make of this episode? The night manager's brother and the lady both could see the ghostly presence (although they were the only ones who could). They were in agreement not only about what took place (where the presence was, the look on his face, and so on) but about his appearance, right down to his Vandyke beard. However, though the manager's brother could see the Man in Gray, he could not see the flight of stairs or the woman at the top. The lady who had seen her compared the woman to Gloria Swanson, complete with a fox boa, a satin hat with a black band across the forehead, and elbow-length gloves. As to the Man in Gray, he was described as about 5' 10" tall, of medium build, and wearing a salt-and-pepper suit with a black tie. Although the night manager could see neither of the ghosts, he said he did feel the Man in Gray's presence and could hear him talking.

As for me, I felt nothing, saw nothing, and heard nothing. Yet I can't help but feel that *something* was there, because the lady seemed to be definitely "in tune" with more than her imagination.*

---

* Moreover, those who hear the tape—even those who claim to be nonbelievers—are in most cases convinced that this was one of those rare occasions when *something of the supernatural* did take place! (For a follow-up to this account, see "His ghostly presence was with them," page 121.)

# There is something unusual about the place . . .

*March 6, 1984*   While rummaging through a stack of Monterey Peninsula publications, I ran across the October 1977 issue of *This Month* magazine, which contains the article written by El Frieda and Herbert Liese (see "They heard rumbling noises," page 34). Upon rereading the article I was reminded that the guide who led the writers through the building was an "unquestioned skeptic" as far as ghosts were concerned. For several years this seemed to be the norm for guides who worked in the building, who were evidently reluctant to admit that there might be more to the structure than Robert Louis Stevenson memorabilia. The authors, however, maintained an open mind. After doing some research on their own, they stated, "No matter how much the skeptics scoff at the ghost stories that have grown up around the Stevenson House . . . one has to admit there is something unusual about the place." In summing up their findings, they write, "So who is to say there are no ghosts at the Stevenson House? There's something!"

# The woman had vanished . . .

*March 8, 1984*   A column in today's *Monterey Peninsula Herald* discusses the Stokes Adobe and its ghosts (see "All the crystals tinkled in unison," page 112). The building is in the midst of a major renovation, as a new restaurant is about to make its debut. Apparently the ghost (or ghosts) also has a bit of finishing work to do. When workmen arrive in the mornings, they discover that their tools have mysteriously been moved!

Another recent happening occurred directly in front of the building. It seems that an older woman darted across the street around 2:30 one morning, straight into the path of an oncoming car. Screeching to a stop to avoid hitting her, the driver jumped from his vehicle to see what had happened—only to discover the woman had vanished! The five witnesses to this event were as befuddled as the driver.

The article mentioned some earlier happenings at the Stokes Adobe, including lights (as well as an elaborate music system) going on in the wee hours of the morning, when no one was in the building; the ghostly figure of a woman whom several late diners observed climbing the main staircase; footsteps that were heard in the upstairs section, when no one was in that part of the building; and the mysterious shaking, pushing, and harassing of workers who were thought to be tapping the till.

## She felt the weight of something on her feet...

*April 20, 1984*  In my book *Ghostly Tales and Mysterious Happenings of Old Monterey* I mentioned a house in the community of Marina that had a variety of ghostly experiences connected with it. Among the happenings were strange noises, shuddering walls, crying sounds, and the "dead weight" of someone (or something) felt by a woman, making it difficult for her to get out of bed. Interestingly, this added happening also concerns one of the building's beds. Approximately ten years after I talked to the woman who shared the original information with me, I had occasion to meet with her again. This update is the result of that meeting.

The story begins with a guest in the house who was planning to spend the night. No sooner had she climbed into her bed (a top bunk) and pulled the covers around her than she felt the weight of something on her feet. Alarmed, she glanced at the foot of the bed. In the darkness she saw what appeared to be a dog. Being afraid of dogs—not to mention ghosts—she threw off the covers and bounded from the bed, hastily departing the room. The commotion woke up the entire household, and in a matter of minutes everyone had congregated in the living room, where they talked about the various events that had been experienced in the building. During this discussion they speculated that perhaps the disturbances were due to the fact that the house (which was relatively new) was rumored to have been built in the vicinity of an old Indian burial ground . . .

## His ghostly presence was with them . . .

*May 25, 1984*  The night manager of the Postgraduate School's dining room facility called me in a state of excitement. The "anniversary lady" had returned to Herrmann Hall and had another encounter with the Del Monte's Man in Gray (see "The Man in Gray pleaded for her help," page 116). The night manager hadn't realized that the woman and her husband, the retired naval officer, were at the facility until it was about time for them to leave. As they briefly chatted, the subject of their previous visit came up. The lady indicated she could remember only a little of what had taken place, as she had tried to block it from her mind. However, she did mention that she thought the Man in Gray had been "speaking through her." She said she was frightened even now, and wanted to get out of the building before the Man in Gray found her.

With that, the three of them started to walk toward the west wing exit. Upon nearing the area in which the previous happening had occurred, both the night manager and the lady again felt the presence of the Man in Gray. Immediately turning around, they decided to head for the building's main entrance. As they proceeded along the downstairs central hall, the presence began to follow them. By the time they reached the Trident Bar (less than halfway down the hall), the feeling of presence had become quite strong, as if it was both behind them and in front of them. Soon they came to a beautiful Spanish-style staircase. Here the presence appeared to leave, as if it had moved toward the steps. Upon seeing the staircase the lady immediately recognized it and said it was similar to the one she had seen during her previous encounter. After passing the steps, they headed for the elevator. By the time they entered the elevator, the presence had returned and was again quite strong. The feeling diminished again while they were in the elevator (perhaps, the night manager suggested, because a second party had entered the elevator with them). However, when they exited the elevator on the second floor (at the west end of the lobby), the presence was as strong as ever. Upon spotting the magnificent main entrance of the old Del Monte, the lady quickened her pace, stating she "wanted to get out of the building." As they neared the door, the presence became very strong, "like it was going past them, through them, and all around them." The ghostly feeling followed them as they hurried through the doorway. At this point the lady turned and told the presence to go back to its room. As it seemed unwilling to leave, the lady turned again and continued toward the front steps—and suddenly collapsed!

Paramedics were called, and the woman soon regained consciousness. When her strength and composure had returned, she was helped to her car. As he watched her and her husband depart, the night manager felt the anger and frustration of the presence, as if it wanted to follow the car. In summing up this account, the manager stated that even though there were times when the presence was extremely strong, he was never able to actually see the Man in Gray. Nevertheless, there was no doubt in his mind that it was his ghostly presence that had been with them.

## Something strange is happening . . .

*May 26, 1984* While visiting the Naval Postgraduate School to make sure I had recorded the latest Man in Gray account accurately (see preceding note), I met a navy pilot who was headquartered there. This man had experienced many things (including flying several combat missions over Viet Nam) and was not the type one would expect to be "spooked" by a ghost. Nevertheless, as we talked about the Del Monte, and all the odd things that had taken place there, he told me about an experience of his own. It seems that he had been awakened in the middle of the night by a "very scary feeling." He felt as if a force was attempting to hold him down and prevent him from getting out of bed. With a shake of his head he added that he hadn't believed in ghosts until he got to the Postgraduate School—"but something strange is certainly happening at the old hotel!"

## The tray abruptly fell to the floor ...

*June 12, 1984*  As I was talking to the manager of the Naval Postgraduate School bookstore, a security guard joined us and shared a couple of her Herrmann Hall experiences. The incident that struck me as the most interesting occurred in the corridor behind the grand ballroom, where several other incidents have been known to take place. According to her story, in the middle of the night when she was alone in the corridor, a tray filled with empty champagne glasses abruptly fell to the floor, breaking all the glasses. How or why the tray tumbled, she can't say ... but she does know that it happened more than once and that the incidents always took place when she was alone.

## The ghost was dressed in a black cap and a gown ...

*July 15, 1984*  An article in the *Monterey Peninsula Herald* told about a ghost who had been observed in an aged frame building near Monterey's Fisherman's Wharf. The structure was once a Chinese gambling club, and—as might be expected—the ghost was of a man of Chinese descent. Old and bearded, the figure was seen late at night walking through an upstairs room. He was dressed in a black cap and a gown that reached to his ankles. The author of the article, Rosalind Sharpe Wall, described him as "gentle and benign" and hinted that he may have been connected with a large quantity of opium that was found about the place.

## The Lady in Lace walked past them . . .

*July 21, 1984*  Over a period of many years the figure of a woman dressed "in flowing robes of lacy white" has been seen in the Pescadero Point area of Pebble Beach (see "The Lady in Lace of Pebble Beach," page 76). The image of the Lady in Lace has most often been spotted near the famed Ghost Tree and has created considerable confusion for motorists who see her walking down the center of the 17 Mile Drive, usually on dark foggy nights. As indicated in my earlier note, one theory suggests that the ghostly figure is Dona Maria del Carmen Barreto, who once owned much of what is now Pebble Beach. However, as more sightings are made, others continue to speculate about the lady's identity. Among them are the couple who told the following tale.

In either 1979 or 1980, the couple were sitting on the rocks at Pescadero Point, overlooking the Pacific. Around 2:00 a.m., a lady "dressed in a long, lacy white gown" walked past them on her way to the shore. Since it was a moonlit night, they were able to see her quite clearly. The couple were unfamiliar with stories of the Lady in Lace and were surprised to see anyone—particularly a lone woman—at that time of night. The dress she wore looked like a wedding gown, and the back of it was dragging in the dirt. As she continued toward the sea, her head was down, and she walked almost as if in a trance. She passed the gnarled remains of an old cypress tree and was soon lost to view behind some rocks. Upon losing sight of her the couple became concerned. Leaving his partner where they had been sitting, the man proceeded to look for the lady to be sure she was all right. As might be guessed, he was unable to find any trace of her.

After learning of the legend of the Lady in Lace, the couple think it was she whom they saw. Incidentally, because of the figure's dress and the sadness she projected, certain people who are familiar with this story have suggested that perhaps the lone walker is a long-ago bride who had been jilted by her lover, rather than a woeful Dona Maria watching over her land.

## The persistent appearance of a beautiful woman . . .

*September 5, 1984*   Here is another in the long list of ghostly happenings associated with Monterey's historic Stokes Adobe (see "All the crystals tinkled in unison," page 112, and "The woman had vanished," page 119). The September 1984 issue of *This Month* magazine mentions a man dressed in clothes of long ago who repeatedly appeared at the head of the stairs after the restaurant had closed and workers were cleaning up. Also experienced by the workers were the sounds of babies crying and the persistent appearance of a beautiful woman in one of the upstairs rooms.

## A ghost haunts its front porch . . .

*October 12, 1984*   While at my favorite Carmel coffee shop I met with Richard Winer, author of *The Devil's Triangle* and co-author of *Haunted Houses*. After we had chatted about ghosts, shipwrecks, and other topics of mutual interest (such as the famed Winchester Mystery House in San Jose, California, where he had had the good fortune of spending a night), he mentioned a "castle" perched on the nearby Pebble Beach shore. Besides boasting an address on the famed 17 Mile Drive, as an added attraction this magnificent mansion has a ghost that haunts its front porch! The apparition has been seen by more than one person. Its identity remains unknown, but it's interesting to note that the structure is on Pescadero Point . . . a stone's throw from the area where the Lady in Lace has most often been seen!*

## Ghosts were said to frequent the place . . .

*October 25, 1984* My book *Ghosts, Bandits and Legends of Old Monterey* mentions an unusual mansion in Pebble Beach made almost entirely of logs. (Unfortunately, the structure was destroyed by fire in 1977.) More accurately described, perhaps, as a country estate, the mansion was gigantic in size. Its living room alone measured 1,800 square feet—the size of many homes. Its dining room was a cube thirty feet long, thirty feet wide, and thirty feet high (as high as some three-story buildings). The building had four huge fireplaces, the largest one boasting an opening eight feet high and twelve feet wide. Built in 1917, the estate was furnished with the best that money could buy, including an elaborate wine cellar stocked with vintage French wines. However, after moving into the mansion the owners stayed only long enough to stage an elaborate dress ball. After this fashionable affair, they moved from the estate— never to return! For more than forty years the dwelling sat vacant. Its only visitors were occasional vandals and a caretaker who watched over the grounds—unless you count assorted ghostly guests who were said to frequent the place.

---

* For more about the Lady in Lace, see "The Lady in Lace of Pebble Beach," page 76, and "The Lady in Lace walked past them," page 124.

Of the number of odd occurrences described as having taken place there, I was able to document only one. This involved a woman who lived in the house with her husband in the 1960s. The woman spoke of hearing a female voice in the house exclaim "Oh, dear!" The voice was "very distinct" and came from a room that had originally been used for luggage, which they had converted to a small bedroom. At the time the incident took place, no one was in the room. In fact, she was the only one in that part of the house. Perhaps, she suggested, the "Oh, dear" she heard so distinctly was the ghost's way of showing her dismay at the changes that had been made.

## They frantically searched every room...

*December 3, 1984* I had an interesting conversation with two individuals who currently work in the Vasquez Adobe (which now houses city offices, as explained in "Shadowy images in a bandit's hideout," page 65). They told me about a man of "about mid-sixty" who had recently stopped by to see whether any changes had been made to the structure. Many years before, he explained, when he was a student at Stanford's Hopkins Marine Station in Pacific Grove, he and a fellow student had lived there. As he was describing what the aged adobe was like at that time, he suddenly paused and asked whether they had ever heard "any strange footsteps." Glancing at each other, the two workers acknowledged self-consciously that they had. Nodding in agreement, the man matter-of-factly stated that the building was haunted. "On numerous occasions," he said, he and his roommate had heard footsteps in the upstairs portion of the house. When this happened they would each run to one of the structure's two staircases and race up the stairs, frantically searching every room . . . but nothing was ever found.

# He always appears in a yellow robe . . .

*December, 1984*   At a holiday gathering, the conversation got around to a picturesque dwelling near Pacific Grove's Asilomar Conference Grounds. (The Conference Grounds overlook the Pacific Ocean and are adjacent to Asilomar Beach. The grounds are situated in a forest setting, amidst rolling sand dunes and twisted pines. The area has been a popular conference site for more than three quarters of a century.) The house this account is about is likewise nestled among the pines and dunes. Resembling something in a picture postcard from the other side of the Pacific, the structure looks as if it had been picked up from the Flowery Kingdom and set down on the shores of the Monterey Peninsula. In light of the many stories that circulate about the building, perhaps this is not far from the truth. Among the tales is an account that states that the house was built in China and shipped (pre-fab style) to Pacific Grove. Other stories say it was constructed for San Francisco's 1939 World's Fair and was brought to the Peninsula by barge when the fair ended. Whatever the case, the house is delightful to look at . . . and it also boasts a ghost! Appropriately, the apparition is an Oriental man. He is said to be quite old and is only seen now and then. He always appears in a yellow robe and has never been known to bother anyone.

# His description matched the Man in Gray . . .

*March 31, 1985*   As I was dropping off books at a Cannery Row store, the clerk told me about an experience his younger brother had at the old Hotel Del Monte. Several years ago, when his brother was in the fourth grade (and long before my book *Incredible Ghosts of Old Monterey's Hotel Del Monte* came out), he visited the Postgraduate School/Hotel Del Monte site on a school field trip. In telling his family about the visit, the boy stated he had had a "strange feeling" when he was in the building. He also said he thought he had seen someone—or something—that wasn't there. Asked what it was he had seen, the brother described an old man. Unbeknownst to him, his description matched the Man in Gray! (See "The Man in Gray," page 80.)

The clerk who told me this story said he found his brother's report to be interesting for a couple of reasons. First, the sighting occurred long before the Del Monte ghost stories became well known. Second, his brother was not the talkative type and spoke only when he had something worthwhile to say. In concluding, the clerk mentioned that his brother had similarly strange feelings—chills, feelings of presence, and the like—in certain other local buildings, including the American Tin Can Company in Pacific Grove and Stillwell Hall at Fort Ord.

## Maybe it was a mirage . . .

*April 5, 1985*   A woman who works for the famed Carmel Bach Festival told me about "a ghost in the auditorium" at Sunset Center. (The internationally known Carmel Bach Festival celebrates the music of Johann Sebastian Bach and has been a colorful part of the village's cultural heritage since 1935. The majority of the performances are held at Sunset Center, which was formerly a school.) Among the things blamed on the ghost are mysterious, high-pitched, bat-like screeches that appear on tapes when the orchestra is being professionally recorded.

A second strange tale from the same source takes us to nearby Point Lobos, slightly south of Carmel. While on a whale-watching excursion off this beautiful promontory, everyone aboard the vessel—"including the guide and captain"—saw what appeared to be a Chinese fishing village on the furthermost section of the point. "Maybe it was a mirage," my informant volunteered, "but whatever it was, it looked real to all who saw it." Interestingly, there *was* a Chinese fishing village at Point Lobos more than a century ago. However, rather than being situated on the promontory, it was located in a small rounded bay known today as Whaler's Cove.

## A woman was killed on or near the back steps...

*June 11, 1985* Even though this account does not directly involve a ghost, it is worth recording as it might help to answer questions concerning the ghostly spirit that frequents the Robert Louis Stevenson House. Those who think the Lady in Black (see "The Lady in Black," page 14) may be someone other than Mrs. Girardin may be interested to learn that an authority on the Robert Louis Stevenson House gives credence to the story that a woman was once killed on or near the building's back steps. According to the story (related in "He drew his blade," page 17), many years ago a woman thought to have been of Indian descent was chased to the rear of the Stevenson House (then known as the French Hotel), where she was killed (probably stabbed). Unfortunately, several questions concerning this long-ago event still remain unanswered. However, the notion lingers that it might be the Indian woman's spirit that haunts the building.

## A mysterious thing in a locked room...

*June 27, 1985* Venturing south from Carmel on the scenic coast road, travelers soon pass an attractive two-story structure. A part of Monterey County history for many years, the building is said to be the scene of several odd occurrences. Among the more common accounts are the somewhat typical tales of doors opening and closing when no one is near them. While this activity apparently occurs in the upstairs section only, the most mystifying of the structure's peculiar events may take place in the basement. Or so the man hinted who told me this tale, saying that there is—or was—a "mysterious thing, or happening, in a locked basement room." Sadly, the who, what, and why of this account may also be locked in that room, as my source didn't know—or wouldn't say—any more.

## He had never seen anything like it . . .

*October 24, 1985*  Around 8:00 a.m. I was walking along the main downstairs corridor of the Naval Postgraduate School's Herrmann Hall. I hadn't gone far when a long-time employee saw me and mentioned that "the ghost" had been seen earlier that morning!

Upon tracking down the person who had told him the tale, I was directed to a gentleman she had spoken with in the Quarterdeck area. After several false leads, I located the individual who had made the sighting.

In sharing his experience with me, my informant took me to the men's dressing room/shower area of the Roman Plunge. (The Roman Plunge is a huge swimming pool that was built in 1918. It was a favorite gathering place for the hotel's guests until the Del Monte closed in the 1940s. Today it is used by Postgraduate School personnel and their families.) Stopping near the showers, he pointed to the spot where he had made the sighting. The image, he said, was "not clear," almost as if it was "in a fog." He went on to say that it was visible only for a few seconds and that he had never seen anything like it before. With a shake of his head, he summed up the episode by saying he didn't know whether what he had seen was a shadow, a reflection, or the real thing.

131

# The figures were almost naked . . .

*December 10, 1985*  Although this account lacks detail, it is worthy of recording because the person who experienced it is a respected Peninsulan. According to his story, while he and a friend were in the vicinity of the Franklin Street entrance to the Monterey Presidio, he saw the ghostly figures of several "almost naked" Indians. This remark was made during a discussion of the Presidio and of some rather odd occurrences that have taken place there. Unfortunately, I was unable to question the man further about the incident. What makes his story particularly interesting is that the remains of an aged Indian village have been found on the Presidio grounds—and that the Monterey Indians are known to have worn very little in the way of clothing.

# A coffin once was stored there . . .

*January 11, 1986*  In my book *Ghosts, Bandits and Legends of Old Monterey*, I mentioned Monterey's Larkin House and a ghostly figure that was said to have been seen in its garden.* The "ghost in the garden" is thought to have been the apparition of a man who was killed there long ago, and whose body was thrown into a well (which is still visible). A human skeleton was also said to have been found in the enclosed yard. This discovery gave rise to rumors that the Spanish had used the area as a burial ground for murdered political prisoners.

All this brings me to a small building that is also located in the garden. In the late 1840s this attractive one-room

---

* Located at 464 Calle Principal, the Larkin House was built by Thomas Oliver Larkin in the 1830s. The first, and only, American consul to California, Larkin lived in Monterey when it was the capital under Mexican rule. The house itself is credited with having pioneered the popular Monterey Colonial style of architecture.

adobe was occupied by lieutenants William T. Sherman and Henry W. Halleck (both of whom were later to become well-known American generals). The building today is known as Sherman's Quarters. Recent research has uncovered an account stating that a coffin was once stored in the structure. Even though the coffin was empty, one only has to let one's imagination wander—particularly in light of the gruesome stories that were told about the garden—to appreciate the type of tales that would circulate about the building and its grounds. Needless to say, most of the children who lived in the area were terrified . . . until the coffin was removed and the building was turned into a billiard room.

## Ghost hunters visit the Stevenson House . . .

*January 11, 1986*  A Robert Louis Stevenson House guide told me about a visit she had had from a small group of "ghost hunters." There were five people in the group, all from outside the Monterey Peninsula area. One of them, she said, may have been more a photographer than a ghost hunter. Before arriving they had called and tried to set up an evening appointment. However, the guide was unable to meet with them after hours, so a private visit was arranged during the lunch hour. As the guide escorted them through the building, they carefully explored each room, feeling doorjambs, doorknobs, and special pieces of furniture. Frequently they closed their eyes and seemed to be deep in thought or concentrating on certain objects. Taking notes as they went, they conferred with each other as they moved about the house. One woman member of the group claimed to see "reflections of the past" in an upstairs mirror. When the guide asked what she saw, the woman invited her to look for herself. But no matter how hard she tried, the guide was unable to see into the past.

Upon completing the tour, the group gathered in the rear garden with the guide to talk about what they had experienced. Among the things the ghost hunters reported were the apparent presence of a "restless spirit" in the upstairs hall (felt by more than one person), organ music in the downstairs entryway (heard by a single individual), the voice of a man and woman arguing on the main staircase (also heard by only one person), and coughing sounds coming from the Robert Louis Stevenson bedroom (again, experienced by a single individual). The guide apparently was not "in tune" with any of what had taken place, since she had been oblivious to all the happenings the group reported.

## A Chinese gentleman was killed . . .

*February 16, 1986*  While enjoying an early breakfast in Pacific Grove, I met an old friend who has been a Monterey Peninsula resident since the early 1900s. Not only has this gentleman seen Bobo (Monterey Bay's mysterious beast of the deep), but over the years he has told me many interesting tales about the way things used to be.* Our breakfast meeting was no exception as far as stories of long ago are concerned, and as we sipped our third cup of coffee he got to talking about ghosts. The most interesting of his accounts concerned a happening that took place near Fisherman's Wharf. Many years ago, long before Monterey's waterfront was transformed into a convention- and visitor-oriented area, a Chinese boardinghouse was in the neighborhood. (The boardinghouse was near the Chinese gambling club mentioned in "The ghost was dressed in a black cap and a gown," page 123.) At this period in Monterey history, a wooden sidewalk connected the buildings. Also at this time a tong war (of sorts) was going on in the area. During this

---

* For information about Bobo and other odd sea creatures, see my book *Shipwrecks and Sea Monsters of California's Central Coast.*

disturbance a Chinese gentleman was killed. For many years afterward people talked about hearing the shuffling sounds of his footsteps on the board sidewalk. Not only were his footsteps heard, but old-timers also told of seeing his ghostly image (queue and all) shambling along the wooden walkway.

## Even though they were happy with the house . . .

*February 16, 1986*  In the 1930s and early 1940s, when Monterey was known as the Sardine Capital of the World, a small frame house was located near the railroad tracks above Cannery Row. At the time this tale took place the dwelling was occupied by a "fishing family." (Today a quality motor inn stands on the site.) Unfortunately, even though the family was happy with the house, they were forced to vacate the premises due to lack of sleep. Surprisingly, it wasn't noise from the railroad, or hubbub from the canneries, that caused the problem. Instead, it was the sound of a baby crying that came from within the structure's walls! No amount of searching revealed the source, and because of the continued crying—coupled with their lack of sleep—the family had no choice but to find a new place to live.

## Hoping to obtain some clue . . .

*March 7, 1986*  While at Monterey's Dixieland Festival I got to talking with one of the officers of the Pacific Grove Heritage Society. In discussing his favorite topic and mine (Victorian houses and ghosts), he said "once or twice a year" people called him who were experiencing strange happenings in the old buildings they were living in. Unable to explain the odd occurrences, they called the Heritage Society for background information on their houses and the people who had lived in them, hoping to obtain some clue as to why the peculiar things were taking place. As he started to tell me about one of the calls, a rousing rendition of "When the Saints Come Marching In" cut our conversation short. As we parted, he agreed to finish the story at a later date (see "Invisible hands were clasped around her throat," page 165).

## The man appeared not to hear her . . .

*April 10, 1986*   After hearing a talk I gave to a local organization, a past employee of the Naval Postgraduate School's kitchen crew approached the podium and began telling me about a happening that had taken place there several years ago. It seems that one evening a waitress was setting up for a party in the La Novia Room when she noticed a man in the adjoining Garden Terrace. (La Novia means "The Bride," and an elaborate glass-encased scene within the room depicts a Spanish wedding procession. The La Novia Room and its adjoining terrace are located on the lower west corridor of Herrmann Hall.) The man was sitting in a chair in front of a roaring fire that had been built in the terrace fireplace. Since no one was supposed to be in either the La Novia Room or its adjoining terrace before the function started, the waitress approached the man and told him the facility was closed and he would have to leave. The man appeared not to hear her or even to be aware of her existence. Since he made no effort to leave, the waitress went in search of other kitchen workers who could help persuade the man that he wasn't supposed to be there. Upon finding two busboys, she hurriedly explained the situation. It was then—as she described the man—that she realized he matched the description of the Del Monte's Man in Gray! (See "The Man in Gray," page 80.) When the three of them rushed back to the Garden Terrace, the room was empty.

136

From that time on the waitress believed in the building's ghosts.

The fellow who told me this tale was one of the busboys involved in the story. To this day he is convinced that the man in the terrace was, in fact, the Man in Gray.

## The ghost of Joaquin Murrieta...

*April 20, 1986* The historic Mission Ranch, located between Carmel Mission and beautiful Carmel Bay, is unique for a number of reasons, among them its hidden treasures, long-lost mines, mysterious tunnels...and ghosts! (Of course, the fact that former Carmel mayor Clint Eastwood currently owns the property does little to detract from its mystique.) Certainly the most famous ghost to have been seen there is that of Joaquin Murrieta—California's best-known badman. Many books have been written about this Mother Lode marauder. Of particular interest to this tale is information indicating that a priest hid him at or near the mission during his reign of terror. Additional information states that the best—and perhaps only—painted likeness of Murrieta was done by a priest while he was in hiding at the church. Why Murrieta's ghost has chosen the Mission Ranch to frequent is anybody's guess, but (with tongue in cheek) it has been suggested he may occasionally pay a call to a female ghost that has been observed in the Mission Ranch bunkhouse, "dressed in an old-fashioned white gown."

## He would find the chairs unstacked...

*May 10, 1986* In 1950 a friend of mine worked at a shoe repair shop in Monterey. While there he met a very distinguished older gentleman who had worked at the Hotel Del Monte during its glorious days before the Great Depression.

During their conversations about the hotel, and what it was like before the government took it over, the older man mentioned many mysterious happenings that had taken place there. One of the events occurred in a room that was used for private parties, banquets, and other special functions. As was the custom, when the function was over the hotel workers would clean the room—stacking chairs, storing items in their proper places, and so on—so that things would be readily available for the next gathering. Being in charge of such affairs, and having the only key to the room, the gentleman who told the tale said he always checked the room after it had been cleaned. Upon satisfying himself that everything was in order, he would lock the room until the next function. However, on more than one occasion, when he opened the room to prepare it for the next gathering, he would find the chairs unstacked and things out of order. Of particular interest to me in this account is the indication that, far from being recent inventions, stories of unexplained happenings have been a part of the Del Monte's history for considerably more than half a century.

## Upon hearing her frantic screams . . .

*May 18, 1986*   As I was autographing books at the Fourth Annual Cannery Row Reunion, an older gentleman stopped by my table. After realizing that I was the author of the Monterey area ghost books, he said he thought he had lived in one of the houses I had written about. With that he proceeded to describe some of the happenings that had taken place there. Among the things he mentioned was a mysterious voice that frequently joined in conversations when two members of his family were talking. Where the voice came from, and who it belonged to, were questions no one could answer.

A second unexplained happening took place in the building's main room. The man himself had experienced this event. He described in detail how a baby grand piano suddenly started moving toward him at a fast pace. Unable to get out of the piano's way, he watched in horror as the instrument nearly pinned him against the wall! However, for reasons he can't explain, the piano suddenly came to a halt, leaving him room to escape.

As if an episode such as this wasn't enough to make the family want to move, the following incident convinced them it was time to vacate the premises. On two occasions the man's daughter awoke in hysterics. Upon hearing her frantic screams, the entire household rushed to her room. There they found a rat that appeared to be drugged lying on her bed near her head! As a final comment about the building, the man said that since his family moved from the house, it has been vacant more often than not. Understandably, no one seems to be able to live there for an extended period of time.

## There was no one upstairs . . .

*July 11, 1986* Over the years the lure of Cannery Row has been as much its people as its buildings. This account involves a mixture of both—or, if not a living person, at least one of the Row's better-known ghosts.

In talking with one of the Row's more colorful characters, I learned about a structure that has been a part of the cannery-lined street for more than sixty years. An important part of the area's history, the building gains additional mystique from the ghost that is said to haunt it. Although the ghostly image has been seen by various people, the diminutive gentleman of Oriental descent seems to appear only when he wants to, and then to only a selected few. Whose presence the ghost represents is not known for sure, but it has been suggested that he is a gentleman who once worked at a dinner house that was located within the structure. The man had lived into his eighties and now his spirit is thought by some to have remained in the area to watch over the building.

Happily for the occupants of the aged edifice, the ghost has let it be known that he is pleased with the restoration work that is being done. And, other than spilling a glass of water down the back of an individual who resides there, he has chosen to be seen rather than felt.

On one occasion the ghost was observed by a woman from outside the area who had stopped by to see a friend who lives in the building. While touring the structure, the visitor became fascinated with the building and its colorful history. She was particularly interested in its rambling upstairs rooms and the many antiques they contained. Desiring to photograph the rooms, she returned the next day. Venturing upstairs, she proceeded to move from room to room, taking pictures as she went. After about two hours she went downstairs and asked her friend who the fellow was that was upstairs with her. Surprised by the question, her friend indicated that she should have been alone. The visitor shook her head and proceeded to describe how, as she was about to photograph a desk topped with old pens, inkwells, and the like, she felt the presence of someone behind her. Turning around, she saw a small Oriental man watching her, dressed in a black cotton suit and black cotton shoes. When he did not respond to her hello, she assumed he could not speak English and continued with her photography. As she went on exploring the various rooms, she said, the man quietly followed her and watched what she was doing.

After hearing the story, the woman who lived in the building realized that it was the ghost that her friend had seen. Not knowing how her guest would react, somewhat hesitatingly she told her about the ghostly presence. Far from being alarmed, her friend commented, "He's adorable!"—and promptly went back upstairs to finish her photography.

# A wine glass was lifted from her hand . . .

*July 17, 1986*  Not at all shy about ghosts, the management of the restaurant housed in the Stokes Adobe* hints that the presence who frequents the front upstairs (balcony) room is that of a "socially prominent" woman who lived in the building for nearly sixty years. This information, along with other bits of local lore, is documented on the back of the restaurant's menu.

Also of interest in connection with the Stokes Adobe is the information I gained from a knowledgeable employee there. Among his many tales was the account of a woman who was attending a function in a small downstairs party room. Suddenly a wine glass was lifted from her hand and transported part way across the room before it fell to the floor. According to the employee, several bewildered people witnessed the event.

A second object that moved on its own was a candelabra. This took place in the bar section of the building. As stated by the employee, for no apparent reason the candelabra suddenly slid across the top of the piano and fell to the floor! No one was near it when it took its short journey, but there were a number of customers in the bar who saw it slide and crash to the floor. Add in the cold spots experienced in one of the upstairs rooms, and one has to admit this aged adobe has a place of honor among the many Monterey Peninsula buildings that are known for their tales of the strange and unexplained.

---

* For more Stokes Adobe stories, see "All the crystals tinkled in unison," page 112, "The woman had vanished," page 119, and "The persistent appearance of a beautiful woman," page 125.

## Stevenson's presence has been seen in the ruins...

*July 18, 1986*  Those who feel cheated because the ghost (at least the best-known ghost) at Monterey's Robert Louis Stevenson House is not that of the famed Scottish writer may be interested in knowing that his presence has supposedly been seen at the ruins of an old ranch house in Carmel Valley's Robinson Canyon. The ruins are of the structure in which Stevenson was nursed back to health after he was found "nearly dead" in the rugged foothills of the Santa Lucias. Several stories have been told about this episode in Stevenson's life, with at least one source indicating that it was this brush with death that prompted him to write his poem "The Requiem."*

## A strong feeling of pain and tears...

*April, 1987*  According to the local publication *Coasting*, one of Pacific Grove's most delightful inns boasts a disturbing spirit that seems to come and go. The inn is a large, beautifully restored Victorian building, located in the heart of the Grove. Apparently the ghostly presence is most often felt in the upstairs section, as guests who frequent a particular room have reported an "aura" that "put them on edge." One overnight visitor even spoke of "a strong feeling of pain and tears" that emanated from the room.

## The elevator was empty...

*April 30, 1987*  While attending a meeting at the Naval Postgraduate School, I learned of another ghostly sighting

---

*Stevenson sent this poem to his literary adviser, suggesting that it be used as his epitaph. Three years after his death a plaque bearing the poem was placed on his tomb in Samoa.

at Herrmann Hall. What makes this account different from most of the others is that the ghost was a woman rather than the more familiar Man in Gray.

According to the gentleman who told the tale, a courier who worked for the Postgraduate School was walking toward the elevators at the west end of the lobby when he saw a slender woman with blonde hair enter one of them. The woman was striking and wore a long, form-fitting, white gown, complete with gloves that reached to her elbows. As she pushed the button for her floor, the elevator door began to close, blocking her from view. The courier quickened his pace, hoping to catch the elevator before it moved, and reached the door just as it clicked shut. Hastily he pushed the button, and the door immediately opened. Upon peering in, he discovered that the elevator was empty!

I find this account interesting for a number of reasons, among them the source from which it came (a respected, long-time Postgraduate School employee) and the fact that the ghost was a woman. I can't help but wonder whether the lady observed by the courier was the "woman at the top of the stairs" who was seen by the wife of the retired naval officer (see "The Man in Gray pleaded for her help," page 116) . . . and who was described as wearing elbow-length gloves!


## It took their breath away . . .

*June 5, 1987*  This story properly begins back on June 22, 1970. On that day I talked with the guide at Monterey's Robert Louis Stevenson House and heard many interesting tales about the old building. Among the stories was a brief account about the smell of carbolic acid in the room Stevenson was thought to have stayed in. (In days of old, carbolic acid was often used in sickrooms as a disinfectant.) With Stevenson having been ill while staying in the building,

I thought this was of interest and mentioned it in my book *Ghosts, Bandits and Legends of Old Monterey*. Now, seventeen years later, I was visiting a local woman while tracking down information on south Monterey County's Los Burros Mining District. (Her father had been connected with the district and was mentioned in my book *Monterey's Mother Lode*.) When it was about time for me to leave, the lady said she enjoyed my writing and had many of my books. With that she went on to say I had even written about her in my first ghost book. Surprised by her comment, I asked which account she was connected with. It was then that she told me that it was she who had smelled the carbolic acid!

In the late 1960s, the woman explained, she and her sister visited the Robert Louis Stevenson House. Upon venturing upstairs (visitors were allowed to tour the building at their own pace at this time), they made their way to the Stevenson bedroom. While standing at the railing (designed to prevent people from getting too close to the furnishings and the Stevenson memorabilia), my acquaintance began thinking about Stevenson's stay in Monterey and the many stories she had heard about the house. After a time, when only she and her sister were in the room, she got up her nerve and said out loud, "Robert Louis Stevenson, if you're around, will you move some of these things." At the exact instant of her request, she went on, "a sort of swoosh" filled the room! In describing the sensation, the lady shut her eyes and said, "It was like a pressure that circled us; it was an extremely cold wind." Opening her eyes, she went on to say that besides chilling them, the wind had "the smell of carbolic acid" in it. Indeed, the wind and its smell of medicine were so strong that "it took our breath away." Terrified by what was taking place, her sister ran from the room—high heels and all—and didn't stop until she reached the guide's desk near the building's entrance. My informant stated that she wasn't as frightened as her sister, because she had experienced other odd occurrences during her life.

Eventually she also left the room and made her way down-stairs to rejoin her sister. The building's guide, having lis-tened to their tale, proceeded to tell them about several other strange happenings that had taken place within the building.

This fascinating account prompts me to note a point of interest to people who wonder about tales of mysterious happenings. Over the years I have heard hundreds of second-hand ghost stories and tales of the supernatural. Like anyone, I often wonder how many of these accounts are based on actual happenings. Every so often, however, an incident like this one occurs, and I have the opportunity to speak with the person who actually experienced the event. At such times I realize that even though many of the accounts may be exaggerated, they often are based on inci-dents that did, in fact, take place.

## Indications of the famed author's presence . . .

*June 5, 1987* After jotting down the story of the smell of carbolic acid in the Stevenson House (see preceding note), I taped an aged article from the *Monterey Peninsula Herald* to the page to remind myself that other individuals may also have experienced indications of the famed author's presence. Specifically, the article states that a curator at the building in the late 1950s heard a heavy object being dragged across the upstairs floor. Even though she was (supposedly) alone in the house, she bravely ventured upstairs to investigate. There she found a heavy trunk (which is said to have belonged to Stevenson) in the hall out-side the room it was usually in. This, plus the mysterious movement of books in the Stevenson bedroom, prompted the curator to think the author's ghost was about.

Nor was the curator the first person who may have experienced the presence of Stevenson's ghost. According to the article, Mrs. Lloyd Osbourne, the wife of Stevenson's stepson, reportedly had visitations from the author after his death. The article also states that while on her deathbed Stevenson's mother said, "There is Louis! I must go."

## She passed right through the wall...

*September 10, 1987* Downtown Monterey once boasted a large hotel known as the San Carlos. (The Monterey Sheraton Hotel now occupies the site.) Built in 1925, the nine-story San Carlos was the Peninsula's most visible landmark for nearly sixty years before being demolished in 1983. During its reign it catered to countless celebrities, including many of Hollywood's best-known stars.

The ballroom at the old San Carlos is where this tale takes place. It was related to a member of one of my college extension courses by a long-time resident. At the time of the event, the ballroom was divided in half, with functions going on in both sections. Young people were "rockin 'n rollin" in one room, while next door a more traditional type of dance was taking place. With two bands playing, and both dance floors crowded, a woman dressed in a white, wedding-like gown mysteriously appeared in the center of the traditional dance floor. For no apparent reason, she started walking toward the wall that divided the ballroom. As people parted to let her through, she walked up to the wall—and passed right through it, without slowing her pace! The music and dancing in both rooms came to an abrupt halt as people stared in astonishment. The woman continued to the center of the second dance floor, whereupon she turned and walked out of the room. Upon reaching the hotel lobby, she headed for the main entrance and suddenly vanished from view!

## Stories of ghosts that haunted the house . . .

*September 10, 1987*  As recorded elsewhere in these notes, stories of ghosts at Monterey's Robert Louis Stevenson House have been with us for a long time. The following account adds credibility to this statement, as it was obtained—without any prompting—from an elderly woman who was born on the Peninsula in the 1890s.* When she was very young, the woman recalled, her father owned a bakery in the heart of Monterey. Among her childhood duties was delivering baked goods to some of his downtown customers. In describing the deliveries, she said that whenever she had to go to the Stevenson House, she would run up and down the steps as fast as she could because of stories she had heard about ghosts that "haunted the house."

## The cause of death was consumption . . .

*September 10, 1987*  Point Sur rock has been a landmark for navigators since early explorers first charted the California coast. In 1889 a lighthouse was built on the massive rock promontory. But, as the Golden State continued to grow, and as its shipping lanes became more and more crowded, not even the powerful beam of the Point Sur light, or the mournful cry of its foghorn, could keep all the ships away from the rugged coast. Many ships—and lives—were lost in these mishaps. However, it's not the ghosts of shipwreck victims that this note is about. Instead, it's about the lightkeeper's house perched high atop the rock. Built of stone and standing three stories high, the imposing structure is visible from California's scenic Highway One about

---

*Like the preceding account, this story was recorded by a member of one of my college extension courses, who contacted and interviewed the elderly woman.

nineteen miles south of Monterey. Among the tales connected with the house are stories of coughing sounds that
came from a third-floor bedroom. The dry, hacking cough
occurred when the room was empty, and those who heard
the disturbing sounds agreed that the cough came from a
woman. In checking into the history of the house, a past
resident learned that around the turn of the century a
woman of about eighteen died in the third-floor room. The
cause of death was consumption!*

## A ghostly image floats down the stairs . . .

*September 10, 1987*   A combination of sources—including
an extension course report and a newspaper article from
1973—suggest there are ghosts at Monterey County's historic
Paraiso Hot Springs. Paraiso Hot Springs is approximately
twelve miles southwest of the Salinas Valley town of Soledad.
Around the turn of the century it was considered one of the
most famous resorts of its kind in the West. According to the
above-mentioned sources, a cabin at the facility is said to be
haunted. Among the manifestations associated with the
dwelling is the ghost of a woman who floats down the stairs!
The area around a second cottage, and a nearby tree, have
also been referred to as places where odd things take place.
Included in the happenings are the sounds of voices and footsteps when no one is around to account for them. Fortunately
for those who frequent the area, the ghosts are not the type
to create any problems. Except for the shock of seeing a
ghostly image float down the stairs, the experiences are
described as being of the pleasant variety.

* This tale came to me in a rather roundabout way. It was reported by one
of my extension course students, who had learned of it from a researcher
for the State of California. The researcher, in turn, had heard it from a
former Point Sur lighthouse keeper. On more than one occasion, a member of the lightkeeper's family is said to have heard the distinct coughing
sounds.

# A cool mist enveloped the graveyard . . .

*September 10, 1987*   This eerie story was taken in part from an account that was recorded by one of my extension course students. He had heard it many years before from an old man in south Monterey County. It is similar to stories that are told in various parts of our country, most of which have been adapted to the vicinity they are told in. Perhaps the story is an example of such tales. However, it is unfair for me to prejudge it, since I did not talk to the person who experienced it. Certainly it has a place in local lore. I will let others judge whether it might be true . . .

Said to have taken place in 1925, the tale begins with two men who were in their early thirties. They were good friends and had visited the downtown area of Salinas, where they drank a few beers and danced with the local ladies. When it was time to leave, they began their long walk home. After a short distance they parted, each taking the shortest route to his house. The path one of them took led through the Salinas cemetery. As he made his way through the graveyard, he became tired and stopped to rest. The spot he chose was under a big tree, with tombstones all about. It was not long before he began to feel like he was not alone. Turning around, he saw a girl who appeared to be in her mid-teens. Not knowing what to do, he somewhat self-consciously introduced himself. She, in turn, told him her name and said she lived with her parents a short distance away. As she talked, a cool mist enveloped the graveyard, and he saw her shiver in the night air. Realizing she must be cold in her light clothing, he took off his jacket and offered it to her. Thanking him for the jacket, she gave him her address and told him he could pick it up the next day.

Late the following morning the man stopped by the girl's house to get his jacket. His knock on the door was answered by an elderly couple. After he introduced himself and explained why he was there, they invited him into their small house. As they listened to his account of the night

149

before, the lady started to sob, while her husband reached for a framed photo that was nearby. With tears in his eyes he showed the picture to their guest. As soon as the visitor saw the photo, he said it was the same girl he had seen the night before. It was then that they told him the picture had been taken on her fifteenth birthday. That was in 1910, the day before she drowned while trying to cross the Salinas River!

After drying their eyes and getting control of themselves, the elderly couple accompanied the man to the cemetery. There, under the very tree he had stopped to rest, the couple pointed to their daughter's grave . . . where, neatly folded on top of the tombstone, was his jacket!

## The kimono-clad ghost . . .

*November 21, 1987* As I was autographing books at the Naval Postgraduate School, an older woman purchased two of my children's books. While I was signing them, she shared a ghost story with me. It seems that her parents had purchased a house in Carmel's picturesque Carmel Point area. They bought the structure from the original owner, a large woman who was in the habit of wearing kimonos. Included in the sale was much of the building's furniture. As the story goes, one night a friend from San Francisco was put up in the guest room. In the middle of the night the visitor awoke from a sound sleep to see a large woman—clad in a kimono—standing in front of the dresser, going through one of the drawers. Frightened by the sight, the visitor rushed from the room (causing the intruder to depart) and frantically woke up the other occupants of the house. Upon listening to her account, the owners realized that her description—right down to the kimono—matched the woman from whom they had purchased the house! Not knowing what she had been looking for, the couple took a picture of her from a drawer and put it on the dresser. From that time on they had no further visits from the kimono-clad ghost.

# The man was wielding an axe . . .

*December 18, 1987*   I heard this account while autographing books at Colton Hall during Monterey's annual Christmas in the Adobes tour. (Located in the heart of old Monterey, Colton Hall was the site of California's constitutional convention in 1849.)

The incident happened during Fleet Week in May of this year, when the battleship *Missouri* visited Monterey Bay. Among the personnel who helped with the proceedings was a naval officer who had been briefly assigned to the Naval Postgraduate School. While at the facility he was quartered in the main building's historic west wing. (The east and west wings adjoin Herrmann Hall. They were constructed in 1888 and survived the Hotel Del Monte's disastrous 1924 fire.)

One night while the officer was asleep in his room, he was awakened by a frightening experience. In recounting the event he told of a man running through the room, attired in a coat similar to what a firefighter would wear, complete with ashes on his arms and shoulders. The man was wielding an axe and was in pursuit of a woman who was wearing a bridal gown!

Although it was clear that no one was actually there, the officer was disturbed by how real the scene seemed. The next morning, he was on duty at the Monterey breakwater, helping to oversee the launches that were transporting visitors to and from the "Mighty Mo." Still disturbed by the events of the night before, the officer told a fellow worker, a navy pilot, about the incident. Upon hearing the story, the pilot (who was familiar with some of the Del Monte's ghost stories and who later shared this account with me) nodded in understanding and told the officer about some of the other ghostly happenings that had taken place at the facility. After hearing these tales, the visiting officer was understandably quite shaken.

151

# A potpourri of ghosts . . .

*March, 1988* I taught a short course this month for the popular Gentrain program at Monterey Peninsula College. The class was made up mostly of adults who lived in the Monterey Bay area. As in many of my classes, I asked the participants to seek out individuals who had lived in the area for lengthy periods of time and to record one or more of their tales about the way it used to be. Of course, with many members of the class being long-time residents themselves, if they wished to share some of their own experiences, that was okay too. The following potpourri of tales contains brief summaries of four of their reports. Among other things, these accounts again illustrate that interviews are a wonderful way to record and preserve interesting bits of local lore.

1. One student wrote of her own experience at the Robert Louis Stevenson House. One warm and sunny day she was in the yard of the Stevenson House, waiting for her tour to begin. While strolling about the garden she came to a shaded spot that seemed unusually cold and quiet. She felt "as if time had slipped back to another era." However, she did not linger there for long, as the door to the Stevenson House opened, signaling that her tour was about to begin. As she followed several people into the building, she glanced at the main staircase and saw a woman dressed in black start down the stairs. Thinking it was the guide, she was impressed with the authenticity of the woman's costume. As the group slowly funneled into the next room, she again glanced at the stairs, only to discover that the woman had disappeared!

Later, when the visitors ventured upstairs, she experienced the same coldness she had felt in the garden as she neared the top of the stairs. At this time "strange little shivers" ran up and down her neck, and she felt an invisible presence pass her on its way down the stairs. In summing up her account, the woman wondered whether it was the

Lady in Black that she had seen and felt (see "The Lady in Black," page 14). She added that at the time the incident took place she was unaware of the Stevenson House ghost and did not believe in such things.

2. Another Stevenson House sighting was reported by a second member of the class. This event occurred in the late 1940s and was experienced by a woman who has been a long-time resident of the area. The incident took place one summer day when she was taking her children to some of Monterey's historic buildings. Shortly after entering the Stevenson House, she experienced an uncomfortable feeling and decided to leave. As she was on her way out, she glanced at the main staircase and saw a woman in a long, dark skirt standing near the top. The woman wore black shoes, and her dark brown hair was pulled into a bun. When the visitor mentioned the woman to the guide, he indicated that no one could be there, since the visitor and her children were the first—and only—guests of the day! As with the preceding account, it wasn't until later that the visitor who saw the mysterious woman learned that there was a famous ghost at the Robert Louis Stevenson House.

3. According to a third report, an aged Carmel Valley adobe was once the scene of "bloodcurdling" screams. The screams took place at night and were frequently followed by a mysterious light that created ghostly shadows within the rooms. There are a number of theories about who—or what—was responsible for these events. One tale tells of a previous owner who had a leg amputated while strapped to a table within the building (the amputation was due to an accident with a bull). According to the story, the leg was buried near the adobe, and after the gentleman died, his ghost returned to the area in hopes of retrieving it! However, others who are aware of the strange sights and sounds think they have nothing to do with ghosts. Instead, they are of the opinion that the cries came from mountain lions that were upset by the lights of passing cars, which in turn created the spooky images in the rooms. (Mountain lions are known

to have frequented the area, and the lights of the cars are said to have interrupted their hunting.) As an addendum to this tale, it has been said that a number of well-known California badmen (including Joaquin Murrieta, Three-fingered Jack, and Tiburcio Vasquez) hid out in the Carmel Valley adobe when it was abandoned. Who knows, maybe the bloodcurdling screams that have been heard are cries from the victims of these long-ago villains.

4. The events in this tale took place in 1937, as a friend of the poet Robinson Jeffers was in the process of photographing sections of the Santa Lucias that Jeffers had described in his works. The photographs were intended for a book of Jeffers' poems, in the hope that they would help readers appreciate both the poetry and the grandeur of the coastal mountains. One gray day, as the photographer drove south from the Monterey Peninsula on scenic Highway One, he pulled to a stop near Mal Paso (Bad Crossing) Creek. Gathering his equipment, he made his way through the fog and began climbing up a ridge. Birds chirped and cows watched intently as he struggled through the wet grass. However, as he rose above the fog and gazed out over a sea of clouds, all sounds suddenly ceased. Even though the unnatural silence made him uncomfortable—almost as if he was being watched—he continued up the ridge to the rock formation he wished to photograph. Here he set up his equipment, including his camera, tripod, and black camera cloth. Upon ducking under the cloth to prepare for the picture, he felt a nearby presence. But, even though he frequently peeked out from under the cloth, he could see nothing out of the ordinary. Still, the longer he stayed in the area the stronger the presence became. Finally he could stand it no longer, and gave in to an overwhelming desire to get off the ridge. Quickly gathering his equipment, he hurried to his car. Who or what was watching him, he could not say, but he felt certain that *something* was there.

Later he shared his experience with Una Jeffers (Robinson's wife). She showed "no surprise," stating matter-of-factly, "Oh, you saw the Little People." In fact, the photographer hadn't *seen* anything, but he *had* experienced something strange in the Santa Lucias. (The fact that this episode took place in the 1930s is of more than passing interest to me, since it was in the 1930s that the previously mentioned works of Steinbeck and Jeffers—both of which hint of strange beings in the Santa Lucias—were published. See "The dark watchers of the Santa Lucias," page 102.)

## He was tipping his hat as people passed ...

*March 2, 1988*   While helping to escort a group of fourth-graders to Monterey Bay's harbor community of Moss Landing (where they were to board a replica of Francis Drake's ship, the *Golden Hinde*), I had the pleasure of sharing my bus seat with a delightful little lady whose father (a Marine) was attending the Naval Postgraduate School. As we chatted the subject of ghosts came up, and she volunteered the information that her dad thought he had seen the Man in Gray. When observed, he "fit the description" so many have given—and was tipping his hat as people passed

## An older man appeared beside them ...

*March 16, 1988*   During an early morning coffee stop I met with a Monterey policeman who shared an interesting account with me. It seems that a fellow police officer was recently married at the Naval Postgraduate School chapel, with the reception taking place in the ballroom. In attendance were several local policemen. Among the group was an officer who had worked at the Postgraduate School when he was a teenager and experienced several ghostly happenings there. Over the years he had related some of his experiences to his friends and to fellow policemen. While he and a second officer were in the ballroom (near a door that led to an inner corridor and the upstairs kitchen) enjoying the festivities—which included a rather loud band—the figure of an older man dressed in gray appeared beside them. Looking at the officers, the man said, "Will you please keep quiet in my house!" Shocked by the figure's sudden appearance—and its equally baffling disappearance—the policeman who had only been told about the Man in Gray (see "The Man in Gray," page 80) blurted to his friend, "It was the ghost, wasn't it?" The first officer responded by telling his companion not to talk—"Don't discuss what we've seen with anyone!"—and went to get something to write on. Upon his return he handed a piece of paper and a pencil to his friend and said, "Write what you saw, everything you can remember." With that he did the same. When they compared notes, they found that their descriptions matched—and that each depicted the Del Monte's mysterious Man in Gray!

## The phantom priest . . .

*May, 1988*  Another extension course . . . and another ghost story. After I shared some interesting accounts about the Royal Presidio Chapel and its old rectory with members of my class, one of the students (a teacher himself) told the following tale.

In the early 1960s, when he was in a high school religion class, the instructor, a Catholic priest, discussed a strange happening he had experienced while visiting a fellow priest in Monterey. Early one morning the instructor awoke from a restless sleep, dressed, and ventured out of the rectory into the darkness. Seeing a dim light coming from the Royal Presidio Chapel, he decided to investigate. Upon entering the church through the side (priest's) entrance, he heard "mumbling" sounds and noticed that the altar candles were lit. Walking toward the altar, he suddenly stopped and stared in awe. In front of him was the "image of a priest saying mass"! Not only did the image move as it conducted the service, but pages of the altar missal (the large book containing prayers and scripture readings) turned when the image was close to it. After watching the phantom priest for several minutes, the instructor hurried out of the chapel to get his friend. Unfortunately, when they returned, the church was empty. However, even though the image was gone and the candles were out, it was obvious that the candles had been lit—and the altar missal was still open!

## A strong feeling of presence . . .

*June 15, 1988* An aged building in the Cannery Row area that currently houses one of Monterey's favorite restaurants once radiated a strong feeling of presence. The feeling was experienced by only a few people, and then only on certain occasions. Among the times the presence was most noticeable was when the establishment first opened. Baffled and concerned, the owner decided to have the structure checked out by two individuals who deal in such things. These people reportedly picked up "strong vibes" (feelings of presence) and indicated that two people had died in the building. One death was said to have involved an elderly alcoholic man who was thought to have stayed in the structure before it was renovated. Supposedly the person "coughed a lot" and died an "alcoholic's death" (whatever that may mean). The second individual was thought to have been murdered in the building long before it became a restaurant. Happily for the owner, and for those who dine in the establishment, the presence has long since departed, and those who frequent the premises can concentrate on fine food and wine rather than "spirits" of another kind.

## More odd happenings at the Hotel Del Monte . . .

*July 29, 1988*  After giving a talk to the Officers' Wives Club at the Naval Postgraduate School, I had an opportunity to meet with a waitress who had worked at the facility for many years. In discussing odd happenings at Herrmann Hall, she shared two stories with me. The first incident took place in the early 1980s and involved a fellow worker, a man of about sixty who was also a long-time employee at the facility. He was vacuuming in the El Rancho Room, a downstairs dining area, when the event occurred. Sometime between midnight and 1:00 a.m. he glanced up from his work to see a small gentleman with gray hair, a gray beard, and a gray suit walking down the hall, past the El Rancho Room entrance. Because it was so late, and visitors were not supposed to be wandering about the building at that hour, the worker thought the man might be lost and turned off the vacuum to see whether he could be of help. Approaching the entrance with the vacuum still in hand, he was shocked to discover that the visitor had disappeared! Frightened by what had taken place, the worker dropped the vacuum and ran from the room. Upon reaching the night office he was as white as a sheet and very unnerved. After reporting the incident to his superior, he quit his night job then and there (though he agreed to continue working at the facility during the day). In summing up the account, the waitress said that if the man had not worked at the Postgraduate School for so long and been such a trusted employee, she wouldn't have put so much faith in his report. However, after talking to him about the happening, she is convinced he saw the Del Monte's mysterious Man in Gray (see "The Man in Gray," page 80).

The waitress's second story is about an incident that occurred in the La Novia Room, also in the early 1980s. In the company of a second waitress (who had also worked at the facility for many years), my informant was setting up the room for a wedding reception. Included in the setup was a long table placed in front of the La Novia (Spanish wedding procession) scene. Atop the table was a large wedding cake with an ornate candelabra on each side. Suddenly, when no one was near the objects, one of the candelabras began to rock briskly from side to side! Nothing else on the table moved, including the second candelabra. As the rocking continued, the two waitresses exchanged bewildered glances, each wondering what could be causing it. Perhaps, thought the waitress who shared the tale with me, a low-flying airplane had created vibrations strong enough to rock the candelabra. However, there were no low-flying airplanes at the time. (People familiar with the Naval Postgraduate School and the flight patterns of the nearby Monterey airport will appreciate this theory.) The waitress also wondered whether an earthquake was to blame for the movement, but no earthquakes were reported in the following day's newspapers. Further, only one of the two candelabras had moved. To this day the waitress wonders who or what caused the candelabra to rock . . . and to this day she gets "eerie" feelings when she works in some of the rooms after dark.

## A ghostly image quivered in the window . . .

*August 11, 1988*   A pizza parlor in Monterey is the setting for this tale. Supposedly several strange happenings have taken place there over the years. Among the events are benches that have been moved across the walkways and entrance when no one was in the building, the sighting of a ghostly figure within the restaurant and a neighboring store, and a sudden picture loss on the television screen after a mysterious figure was seen lurking nearby. The most interesting account that was shared with me took place in 1987 and involved four people. While enjoying a pizza the foursome saw the "quivering" image of a man "suspended

159

in air" within the framework of the front window. The pizza-eaters were so unnerved that they rushed from the restaurant. Upon discussing the event in the safety of their car, they decided to see whether they could see the image from the outside. With their minds made up they drove to the front of the pizza parlor. Sure enough, illuminated by the lights of the car was the ghostly image, still quivering in the window!

## Sightings at the Monterey Bay Aquarium . . .

*August 18, 1988*   As with several other accounts, it was over a cup of coffee that I heard this Cannery Row tale. Most Monterey Peninsula residents and visitors are familiar with the Row's fabulous Monterey Bay Aquarium. When touring this facility, they learn that it is located on the site of the old Hovden Cannery, one of the first canneries to open in the area, and the last to close. The buildings that house the aquarium were, in most cases, reconstructed, with their outside facades resembling the original structures. The shell of at least one building was saved, however, and it is in this structure that this tale takes place.

One day an aquarium worker exited an elevator and saw an older woman standing in the hall staring at her. The woman was dressed in clothes similar to what the cannery workers wore. Surprised and flustered, the aquarium employee wondered how the lady had got past the receptionist, since all other outside doors are kept locked. When she spoke to the woman in an attempt to find out who she was and what she was doing there, the visitor did not respond. Hurrying out of the hall, the worker went in search of someone who could help the lady out or find out why she was there. When she returned with help, not a trace of the mystery woman could be found.

A second aquarium sighting is perhaps even more intriguing, at least to those who are familiar with the background of the facility. According to the person who related the preceding tale, on more than one occasion the ghostly image of an individual—well known to aquarium workers—has been seen in the crowd. Although several people claim to have recognized the figure and the clothes it was wearing, at this time I do not feel it appropriate to identify the person.

## So unnerving were the happenings . . .

*September 12, 1988*  As he was making the rounds of a residential area in a neighboring Monterey Peninsula community, a policeman saw a young lad move a curtain and peer from the window of a house. Ordinarily this would go unrecorded, but the policeman knew that nobody was supposed to be in the building. He called for backup, and a short time later two officers searched the house. Unable to find the boy, they continued to look around. All appeared to be normal, except for the bedroom where the lad had been seen. In this room they found the closet door open and things strewn about. In continuing their investigation, the officers contacted the person who owned the dwelling. After listening to their story and learning of the clutter from the closet, the owner said that it was because of such things that the house was empty. Others had also seen the boy and had experienced odd occurrences in the building. So unnerving were the happenings that several past tenants had chosen to vacate the premises. Somewhat reluctantly, the owner went on to inform the officers that long before a boy of about ten had committed suicide in the closet of the room where the things were found strewn about!

## He refused to work there ever again . . .

*October 11, 1988*  I stopped by the Monterey Bay Aquarium on my daily walk and had occasion to chat with a gentleman who holds a responsible position there. As our conversation rambled from subject to subject (including such things as the historical importance of the aquarium's colorful murals, expansion plans for the facility, and the fascinating overhead walkways that used to cross Cannery Row), I eventually brought up the subject of the supernatural. Finding my companion both interested in and open to the subject, I mentioned the sighting of the ghostly individual who had supposedly been recognized at the facility (see "Sightings at the Monterey Bay Aquarium," page 160). Nodding, the man told me that the image had been seen several times. One individual, he said, had seen the figure in the upstairs banquet area and was so unnerved by the experience that he refused to work there ever again! Inquiring further about the person who had made the sighting, I was told he "was not the type to dream such things up" and is convinced he saw the ghostly image of one of the aquarium's most respected personalities.

## Coughing sounds at the Stevenson House . . .

*December 1, 1988* While I was autographing books at the Monterey Bay Aquarium's annual holiday gathering, a middle-aged man stopped by my table and began looking through my children's book *The Strange Case of the Ghosts of the Robert Louis Stevenson House.* After reading short sections of the text, he asked whether I had ever heard of the Stevenson House ghost making any noises, such as talking or coughing. I indicated that I was unaware of any such incidents, whereupon he proudly stated, "I have!" He proceeded to tell me that many years before, when people were able to tour the Stevenson House on their own, he had taken his children to visit the building. While they were browsing through the upstairs section, the children soon became bored and let it be known they were ready to leave.

At about this time the man heard coughing sounds coming from an adjoining room. Thinking his children might be disturbing other visitors to the structure, he decided it would be best to go. Making their way down the main staircase, they headed for the exit. As they passed the curator's desk, she thanked them for coming and remarked that it was almost time to close. The man responded that she couldn't close just yet, as there was still someone upstairs. Shaking her head, the curator said that wasn't possible, because all the other visitors had left. With that the man mentioned the coughing sounds he had heard. This prompted an immediate—and thorough—search of the upstairs section . . . but no one could be found.*

## Halloween tales from the *Herald* . . .

*December 9, 1988*  A few days before Halloween, Monterey's Sunday *Herald* printed an interesting article about ghostly happenings in and about the Monterey Peninsula. The article was written by a long-time Peninsulan and *Herald* staff writer. Although my name and some of my stories were mentioned, a number of the tales were new to me. Five such accounts are summarized below.

1. A white ghostly figure was said to have been seen on the hill between Monterey and Carmel. The image was observed by several young Monterey men who were having a bachelor party for one of their friends. After a number of stops in Monterey (presumably at their favorite watering places), the party headed over the hill to Carmel. It was while they were on the Monterey-Carmel road that they

---

*Stevenson House ghost buffs might speculate about the possibility of the coughing sounds coming from the ghost of Stevenson, or of Mrs. Girardin's grandchildren. All these individuals were said to be sick while staying in the structure, and all have been associated with ghostly accounts connected with the house. Unfortunately, the man who heard the coughing sounds didn't specify which room they came from.

encountered the ghostly presence. Tall and glowing, its face cloaked in a hood, the figure pointed a bony finger at them! Terrified, the young men forgot all about Carmel and made a beeline for the Royal Presidio Chapel. Here they roused a priest from the rectory and told him about the faceless apparition. In concluding, the article indicated that the frightened young men sought confession—and that the wedding the next day was quite subdued, as the groom and many of his friends had not yet recovered from the night before. (With several venerable tales discussing ghostly happenings on the old Monterey-Carmel road, one can't help but wonder—as the *Herald* article suggests—whether the ghostly spirits that once frequented the area disappeared when Highway One replaced the road that originally linked the two communities.)

2. Many years ago an elderly woman was often seen standing by the side of a road that led through some artichoke fields near Carmel Mission (now referred to as the Mission Fields area). The sightings always occurred at night. After flagging a northbound motorist down, the lady would gratefully accept a ride. However, as the driver continued his journey and turned to ask where his passenger wanted to go, she was never there! (Perhaps, as was suggested in the previous account, once changes in an area take place the spirits move on. Carrying this thought one step further, I can't help but wonder whether the "artichoke ghost" could be the apparition that has been seen crossing Highway One near the Carmelite Monastery. The image is of a lady, the area remains much the same, and the site is only a short distance from Mission Fields.)

3. This tale tells of a long-ago visitor to the Royal Presidio Chapel's old rectory. Upon ringing the doorbell, the guest was greeted by a priest and escorted to a room near the entryway, where he was told to wait. Eventually a second priest entered the room and was surprised to see someone there. Asked how he had gotten in, the visitor told him about the "other" priest. After listening to the story,

the second priest said, "What other priest? I'm the only one here!"

4. A second brief account about the old rectory mentions ladies from Monterey's Catholic Literature Distribution Guild (who once worked in the building). These women are described as having experienced a number of ghostly happenings at the structure, including encounters with a priest (who was always clothed in an old-fashioned cassock) and a rocking chair that rocked when no one was in it.

5. The *Herald* reporter heard this tale from the Stevenson House worker who experienced it. In discussing ghostly happenings—in Monterey as well as in the employee's native country of Denmark—the worker told of hearing "the sound of large objects being moved" in one of the building's upstairs rooms. A check of the room revealed that no one was in it—and that nothing had been moved. (Similar incidents have been reported by others, with at least one account indicating that pieces of furniture had indeed been moved!)

## Invisible hands were clasped around her throat . . .

*April 23, 1989*  Today is Pacific Grove's twentieth annual Victorian Home Tour. This year also marks the 100th anniversary of the community's incorporation. With these events in mind I decided to visit the Pacific Grove Heritage Society's headquarters (located in a delightful old barn built in 1891). While there I met the gentleman I had chatted with at Monterey's Dixieland Festival (see "Hoping to obtain some clue," page 135). After shaking hands and briefly discussing the successful home tour, he continued where he had left off at the festival and shared a couple of ghost stories with me, both of which concerned Victorian houses in the Grove.

The first account came from a woman who had bought a two-story structure that boasted a Monterey Bay view from the second floor. The beautiful view played a big part in her decision to purchase the property, and she eagerly moved in. However, upon climbing the stairs, intent on relaxing in front of her view window, she felt a tightness around her throat and had trouble breathing. The higher she climbed, the more difficult it was for her to breathe. This was to become a common occurrence, and ultimately her only choice was to remain downstairs. In describing the incidents, the woman said it felt like a pair of invisible hands were clasped around her throat, squeezing tighter and tighter the higher she climbed. Almost at wit's end, and not knowing who she could turn to, the lady called the real estate agent who had sold her the house. Upon visiting the building the agent was forced to admit that he too experienced an uncomfortable feeling while climbing the stairs. Frustrated and scared, the dwelling's new owner decided to rent the house and move into an apartment until things settled down. At last report she was still in the apartment, and the people occupying her Victorian were apparently enjoying the structure . . . including her bay view.

Even though this second account was also unnerving to the woman who experienced it, it leaves us with a feeling more in keeping with Pacific Grove's image of being "the last home town." As already mentioned, the happening occurred in a Victorian, but instead of on a staircase this event took place in a locked bathroom. It seems that the lady of the house was enjoying a relaxing bath when she suddenly sensed she was not alone. Certain that no one could be in the room—she had locked both doors before climbing into the tub—nevertheless she spun around to see a very old woman standing near one of the doors. Dressed in clothes of long ago, the kindly-looking woman somehow seemed to blend with the building. All the same, the lady of the house didn't appreciate company while she took a bath. Reaching for a towel, she hurriedly stepped from the tub. It was then that the ghostly figure approached her with arms outstretched and gave her a motherly hug. Afterward the lady said that an overwhelming feeling of warmth and love swept through her as she was enfolded in the tender embrace.

## The bread was still warm . . .

*May 20, 1989* After a "ghost" talk to the Naval Postgraduate School's Officers' Wives Club, a lady approached the table where I was autographing books and asked whether I had heard about the Hotel Del Monte's old ovens. When I shook my head no, she proceeded to share a somewhat disjointed but interesting tale as I continued autographing books. According to my notes (which I frantically jotted down after the autographing was over), her story went something like this. Some time ago two workers stumbled across a basement room that hadn't been used for years. After looking around, they surmised that it had once been a bakery. Amazed at the aged equipment, and the accumulation of dust, they eventually got around to opening an oven. To their shock, the oven contained two freshly baked loaves of bread! To top it off, even though the oven (like all the equipment) was cold to the touch, the bread was still warm!

## He wonders whether it was a ghost that pushed him . . .

*May 21, 1989* After I gave an impromptu "ghost" talk following the Monterey County Symphony's "Concert in the Park" at the Naval Postgraduate School, a woman rushed up to me and asked whether I was interested in more than just Hotel Del Monte ghosts. Assured that I was, she proceeded to tell me about an experience her husband had had. The incident took place at Monterey's historic old

167

Whaling Station during the city's annual Adobe Tour.* With the building being open to visitors, her husband decided to take a quick look inside while she remained outside with the children. As he was upstairs listening to the guide, somebody—or something—pushed him from behind. Since he was standing at the back of a small group, the man's immediate reaction was that his wife had sneaked up the stairs and given him a push. Whirling around to confront her, he realized that no one was there! Bewildered, and more than a little scared, the man hurried out of the building to tell his wife about the incident. In concluding, the lady said that even though her husband had been a "nonbeliever" before this event, to this day he wonders whether it was a ghost that pushed him.

## The ghostly image of an elderly man...

*June 21, 1989*  While delivering books to the outstanding "Dino-mite" (dinosaur) exhibit at Pacific Grove's Museum of Natural History, I had a chat with two long-time Pebble Beach residents. As they looked through my books, they became interested in the ghost stories and asked whether I had heard about the ghost of an elderly, and quite well known, Pebble Beach man. When I indicated that I was unfamiliar with the story, they proceeded to tell me about several sightings. Apparently the man (a long-time Peninsulan) had lived in a large, old, Spanish-style structure in the heart of the Del Monte Forest (which includes much of the Pebble Beach area). While alive he was known to ramble about his house in a very old and quite shabby bathrobe. Since his death several people have stayed in the structure, and many of them have reported seeing the ghostly image

* For background information and additional Whaling Station accounts, see "He was afraid to go into the room alone," page 46, and "The remains of up to forty people," page 60.

of an elderly man wandering around the house. These people were unfamiliar with the home's previous occupant and unaware of other ghostly sightings. When asked about the presence, they accurately described the building's former owner—right down to his beard and shabby bathrobe! They also indicated that the sightings weren't scary and that the figure only seemed to be interested in shuffling about the house.

## Another aquarium sighting . . .

*July 29, 1989* According to a Monterey Bay Aquarium worker, a second sighting of an aged woman dressed as a cannery worker was recently made (see "Sightings at the Monterey Bay Aquarium," page 160). After seeing the ghostly figure near an office in the original Hovden building, the aquarium employee who made the sighting rushed to her own office and announced she had just seen a ghost! The person who told me this tale was in the office at the time, and said the individual who had seen the image was "as white as a sheet!" The area in which the sighting had been made was immediately checked, and no one could be found. When I asked whether the person who claimed to have seen the ghost was prone to playing tricks, my informant responded negatively, adding that nobody could look as scared as she had without actually having experienced something genuinely frightening.

## A ghost wanders about the shopping mall . . .

*August 3, 1989* Most Monterey County residents are familiar with Northridge Mall in Salinas. However, I wonder how many shoppers who frequent the facility know about a ghostly presence that wanders about the halls at night . . .

This brief hint of a tale was told to me by a woman from Salinas after I gave a talk to one of the local schools. Apparently, long after the mall has been closed the ghostly image of an Indian woman has been seen by workers and security officers. When I asked whether there was more to the story, the lady added that she had heard that part of the complex had been built near an Indian burial ground.

## The sounds of her coughing could be heard . . .

*August 5, 1989*  While visiting the Point Sur lighthouse during its centennial celebration, I got to chatting with one of its docents (an elderly lady who is quite knowledgeable about the lighthouse and its accompanying buildings). When I asked about the ghost that was supposed to have frequented the largest of the stone living quarters perched atop "Lighthouse Rock," she smiled and said that she too had heard the story (see "The cause of death was consumption," page 147). In retelling the tale she stated that around the turn of the century a girl in her late teens lived in the building. Sadly, the young lass contracted tuberculosis (sometimes called "consumption") and died in an upstairs bedroom. The sounds of her coughing were said to have been heard by people within the building long after her death.

## Their ghosts returned to the area . . .

*September 1, 1989*  While three ladies and I were swapping ghost stories in an upstairs office at Monterey's Del Monte Shopping Center, one of the three told about an experience she had had in the Big Sur area (approximately twenty-five miles south of Carmel). At the time of the incident she was living in southern California and had chaperoned a group of teenagers to Monterey County's scenic south coast. Prior to the happening the young people had spent the day hiking and swimming. Exhausted, they climbed into their sleeping bags relatively early and were asleep before midnight. About two in the morning the lady who told the tale was awakened by the sounds of young people laughing and talking. Assuming the noise was coming from the group she was chaperoning, and concerned that they were disturbing others, she hurried to the front porch area, where the sleeping bags were located. To her surprise the teenagers were sleeping soundly even as the sounds drifted away down the hill. Bewildered by the experience, the lady got very little sleep the rest of the night.

The next day she told the old-timer whose cabin they were staying in about what had happened. With a nod and a smile, the man told her not to worry. In days of old, he explained, boy scouts often camped in the area, and every once in a while their spirits returned to relive the good times they had had. "Many a night," he went on to say, "I've been awakened by their presence, and the mischievous goings-on they were involved in."

## The cupboard doors opened and closed . . .

*November 15, 1989*   After hearing a talk I gave in Monterey (among other things, I told several ghost stories), a woman who had attended the gathering contacted my wife and told her about a number of ghostly happenings that friends of hers had experienced. As a follow-up to their conversation I contacted the lady. The incidents, she told me, had taken place in a house near Carmel Beach where her friends had lived for approximately one year. Among the odd occurrences were downstairs cupboard doors that mysteriously opened and closed, as if someone was looking for something. Various other incidents—mingled with a variety of peculiar sounds—occurred in other parts of the house,

171

causing the occupants to think someone, or something, was in the building. However, no one was ever found, nor was anything amiss.

One of the most vivid experiences occurred in the master bedroom. The woman of the house was lying in bed awake when she suddenly felt a presence . . . followed by a tap on the shoulder! Even though this experience was unsettling, to say the least, the woman indicated that she was not frightened and that the presence did not create a bad or mean feeling.

Assorted other noises, as well as feelings of presence, were experienced in the children's room. The adult members of the family felt as if the presence desired to wake the children up so it would have someone to play with.

In checking into the history of the house in hopes of discovering the cause of the happenings, the occupants learned that a young man who had once lived there had been killed on or near Carmel Beach. With this information in mind, one can't help but wonder whether it is his lonely spirit that now haunts the building.

## She never again worked at the Stevenson House . . .

*December 6, 1989*   While visiting Monterey's Boston Store (located in the House of Gold, built in the mid-1840s) I noticed the clerk reading one of my ghost books. Upon being teased about her choice of literature, she smiled and said she had been familiar with many of Monterey's ghost stories long before she read the book. In fact, she added, she had once been a docent at the Robert Louis Stevenson House and may have experienced a ghostly happening herself.

It seems that one day in the 1960s, when she was getting ready for one of Monterey's Adobe Tours, the Stevenson House curator suggested she look through a trunk in the upstairs sewing room for some costume items she was seeking. Upon getting the key to the cell-like door, she and a friend went to the room and proceeded to look through the trunk, which was full of carefully packed costumes and clothes of long ago. Taking what they needed, they put the other items back in the trunk, secured it, locked the door, and returned the key to the curator.

The next day, they again had reason to seek something from the trunk. After obtaining the key they returned to the sewing room and proceeded to go through it, carefully stacking the aged costumes on the floor. Suddenly they came upon an old-fashioned black dress that had not been there the day before. The dress was neatly folded and, unlike the other items in the trunk, it was wrapped in blue (period) paper. When they reported their find to the curator, she was at a loss to explain how the dress had gotten into the room—let alone in the trunk—since no one had been in the sewing room since the ladies' visit of the day before. Because the dress was similar to the costume worn by the building's famed Lady in Black, the woman wondered whether there was a connection between the two.

In summing up her account, the lady who told this tale mentioned that following the Adobe Tour she never again worked as a docent at the Stevenson House. When I asked whether it was the mysterious appearance of the black dress that had prompted her to stop working there, she nodded. It was both that, she said, and a feeling that she was treading where she didn't belong.

## Shades of gray . . .

*February 27, 1990*  A few months ago a friend of mine mentioned a co-worker who experienced a ghostly sighting at the Robert Louis Stevenson House. With my calendar full of book deadlines and lectures, it wasn't until today that I was able to contact her and talk to her about the incident.

According to her account, the happening took place on a gray and gloomy day, and—appropriately—the images she saw also appeared in shades of gray, somewhat similar to an old black and white movie. Among the things that make her report different from most other Stevenson House sightings is her description of two figures rather than one. They were dressed in old-fashioned formal attire, the woman in a skirt that was long and full, the man boasting a handsome top hat to complement his stylish apparel. The pair appeared to be in their thirties and were engrossed in animated conversation as they strolled toward the garden entrance of the downstairs rear parlor. Unfortunately, the sighting lasted only a few seconds—the length of time it took the couple to walk approximately ten paces—which prevented the lady from giving a more detailed description. With this incident having occurred in the mid-1980s, I will end this note with a salute to the elegant ghostly couple and to the haunting happenings that continue to be reported at Monterey's historic Robert Louis Stevenson House.

## Odd things happened after his death . . .

*March 1, 1990*  According to a long-time local resident, sometime during the mid-1980s a relatively young man made his way to the roof of a Monterey hotel. While there he apparently proceeded to indulge a bit too much in spirits of the liquid kind. As the night wore on and as he moved about the roof, he ventured too close to the edge and fell several stories to the ground. Barely alive when he was discovered in the morning, he died shortly thereafter in the hospital.

After the young man's death people who stayed in the suite directly below the spot he had fallen from began complaining of odd things that occurred in the room while they were out for the evening. Aside from furnishings being moved, the majority of the happenings took place in the bathroom. It was here that clothing and toiletries disappeared, only to be found in other parts of the suite (often on the window ledges facing Monterey Bay). People in other rooms—including the quarters directly below the suite, as well as rooms on each side of it—complained of annoying noises, including the sounds of furniture being moved and the toilet constantly flushing. On rare occasions a ghostly figure—thought to resemble the man who fell from the roof—has also been reported by hotel workers. The image is always observed upstairs . . . and always in the middle of the night.

## So intense were the feelings . . .

*March 1, 1990*   While chatting with a Monterey police officer I learned of an aged Peninsula dwelling that had been partially destroyed by fire. Besides burning the second story, the fire took the lives of two people. During reconstruction the building's second story was omitted (allowing space for an attic). Upon hearing noises in the new attic, the occupants of the house called the police. As the responding officer lowered the hinged staircase and ventured up to the attic, he was met by a blast of icy air and an overwhelming feeling of presence. So intense were the feelings that the officer was forced to exit the area. At a later date, police were again called to the house, where they learned that the activities had shifted to the kitchen. Here voices were heard and utensils were taken from the cupboards and drawers. Of added interest at this time were the actions of the family's pet dog. After the reconstruction the animal refused to have anything to do with the attic—and when the happenings moved to the kitchen, it began to avoid that room also. However, when the investigating officer lowered the attic steps to see whether anything was taking place up there, the dog bypassed the kitchen and raced up the steps—perhaps bent on conducting an investigation of its own!

# He saw the lonely figure of the Man in Gray . . .

*March 1, 1990*   I met with the former night manager of the Naval Postgraduate School's dining facility and we got to chatting about the remarkable happening that took place there on the night of February 24, 1984 (see "The Man in Gray pleaded for her help," page 116). During the conversation he matter-of-factly mentioned a member of the Post-graduate School staff he had talked to a few days after the event. After sharing experiences, they realized that *both* of them had seen (or experienced) the Man in Gray on that particular night.

It seems that during the night of February 24 his companion had occasion to be in the area of the La Novia Room. While there he glanced down the corridor toward the west wing (past the spot the earlier event had taken place). To his shock and surprise, he saw the lonely figure of the Man in Gray standing atop the tiled steps!

# The ghost wore overalls . . .

*March 6, 1990*   In following a lead I called a middle-aged woman in Monterey to ask about a ghostly experience she was reported to have had. Upon learning who I was, she became quite friendly and mentioned that more than ten years ago I had autographed two books for her son (one of them about ghosts). With that setting the scene, we had an enjoyable chat, and she proceeded to tell me about a sighting she had made in the early 1980s. Provided that I do not divulge the name or address of the building in which the happening occurred (even though it is city owned), she agreed that it would be alright to mention that it is old, large, and located in a residential section of Monterey.

Over the years many people have reported having "feelings of presence" within this structure, as well as hearing an assortment of sounds. Among the noises were low whistles, the jingling of keys, and water running. Most of the sounds came from the kitchen and bathroom areas. When these rooms were checked, water *was* found to be running, but the sources of the whistling and the jingling keys were never discovered.

As for the lady's own sighting, the incident occurred while she was in the building with a friend. They were standing at the end of a hall when she suddenly felt "they were not alone." Glancing down the hall, she saw the ghostly figure of a man in overalls! Startled by his appearance, she asked her friend to look down the hall and tell her what she saw. Upon seeing the overall-clad figure, her shocked companion "nearly jumped into my arms!" When I asked for a description of the man, the lady said that she could remember only that he was shirtless, wearing overalls, and standing at the opposite end of the hall, looking at them. The figure somewhat resembled a hologram, she said, and it could probably best be described as a ghostly apparition.

As far as my informant knows, there have been no recent sightings in the building, but the noises and feelings of presence continue to occur. As a concluding comment she said that even though the incident gave her "a start," she was less shocked than her friend, because she had seen a ghost once before when she was growing up on the Peninsula.

## He was awakened by the sounds of a party . . .

*March 12, 1990*  While I was enjoying a cup of coffee with a good friend—and half-century resident of Carmel—we got to talking about one of the community's elegant old homes. Today the aged edifice is known for a variety of things, including its architecture, the colorful personalities associated with it, a mysterious "plot" that has been found on its grounds, and a secret room that boasts intriguing tales of the past. Even though I have previously recorded a number of incidents regarding this property (see "A haunted hillside mansion," page 37, and "The sound of the door slamming echoed in her ears," page 44), the story I heard today was new to me. Evidently, a past resident was repeatedly awakened in the middle of the night by the sounds of a party. Music was being played, and people were obviously enjoying themselves. Getting out of bed and following the sounds, the resident was always led to the same upstairs room. As he opened the door—expecting to see a party in progress—all sounds suddenly ceased! Aside from the lights that faded into darkness (as if someone had flipped off the switch), there was no sign of life or any indication that a party had taken place.

## Her hair and clothes are disheveled . . .

*March 12, 1990* A second cup of coffee (see preceding note) brought a second ghost story. This incident took place in the late 1940s and may involve the ghostly figure of a "long-ago-lady" I briefly mentioned in my book *Incredible Ghosts of the Big Sur Coast* (and also touched on in "Halloween tales from the *Herald*," page 163). Early one morning while traveling south on Highway One (in the vicinity of the Carmelite Monastery), my coffee companion and an older Carmel gentleman suddenly came upon the ghostly figure of a woman walking down the center of the road. The figure appeared as they crested a hill and seemed oblivious to the rapidly approaching automobile. As they swerved to avoid hitting the lady (who appeared old, and a bit ragged and windblown), she kept a steady pace and continued down the center of the narrow highway. Shocked by what had taken place, my acquaintance (then a rather young woman) stared out of the rear window as the mysterious figure continued her trek north. Glancing at her companion, who was driving the car, the teller of this tale was surprised at how calm and collected he appeared to be. Frantically she inquired who the lady was and what she was doing there. Her companion replied matter-of-factly that the ghostly image had often been observed in the area, and that he had even seen her several times himself. As to who she was, he indicated no one really knew. However, history buffs know that a small cemetery is located nearby, and old legends tell of a grisly murder that took place in the vicinity long before Highway One wound down the Monterey County coast.

I might add to this account that the frequently observed figure is said to be dressed in tattered clothing, with a shawl or scarf partially wrapped around her head and shoulders. Her hair and clothes are disheveled (as one would expect from the ocean winds), and all in all she is quite ghostly in appearance. If other accounts can be believed, she has been a part of coast history for many years. Finally, although some stories describe her (or a figure similar to her) as crossing the road rather than walking down the center of it, the ghostly image of our "long-ago-lady" was originally spotted long before the incident recorded in this note took place.

## A phantom team of horses . . .

*March 14, 1990*  As coincidence has it the tale I learned today is somewhat similar to the account I recorded a couple of days ago (see preceding note). Both incidents took place south of the Monterey Peninsula on or near Monterey County's scenic coast road, and both resemble tales I recorded in previous publications. In my book *Ghostly Tales and Mysterious Happenings of Old Monterey* I described a long-ago accident involving a wagonload of tanbark that occurred in a rugged Santa Lucia canyon near Carmel Highlands. The mishap resulted in the death of the driver, as both the wagon and team plunged over a cliff and fell to the canyon floor. It was said that for several years after the accident the bells from the collar of the lead horse were heard by passers-by as they neared the spot where the wagon had left the road. The man who told me this tale was in his eighties at the time (1973) and was a native of the area. Unfortunately, I can't vouch for the story, as I didn't hear the bells or witness the wreck, but many of the other tales the old man told me proved to be accurate accounts of the way it used to be.

The story I heard today also came from a Monterey Bay area old-timer (born in the 1920s), a man who is known and respected by people up and down the Monterey County coast. Of special interest is the fact that it also tells of a long-ago accident and ghostly bells. The incident occurred in the Santa Lucias, but instead of a wagonload of tanbark this account is about a coastal stage. Having heard the jingling bells when he was a lad hunting rabbits along the south coast, the old-timer asked his father how such a thing was possible when he was alone in the mountains. Upon listening to his son's story, the dad admitted that he too had heard the bells. It was then that he told his son about an early stage that many years before had wound its way through the coastal wilderness. The stage was equipped with bells so people could hear it coming. On one such trip, when the coach was high-balling down a grade, something frightened the horses. Within seconds both the team and the stage were out of control. In the wild ride that followed the coach tipped over. The accident resulted in the death of one man, thought to have been the driver. After the mishap, his father told him, bells were sometimes heard for years afterward as the stage made its ghostly run along a portion of the old coast road . . . with the figure of the dead driver guiding a phantom team of horses down a never-ending grade.

# The ghost was a baroness . . .

*May 8, 1990* This all started when I was autographing books at a local library. As often happens when my books are on display, the subject of ghosts came up. Soon people began sharing stories with me. The tale that intrigued me the most was related by a gentleman from Pacific Grove. According to his account, his grandmother—a delightful lady who wrote and spoke six languages—had once been a baroness in a far-off country. However, during an upheaval in her homeland, her family (as well as others of similar social standing) were forced to leave. After venturing to various places, she and several other people from her homeland chose Pacific Grove to settle in. Stripped of much of her wealth, she—like many ladies of her day—worked in a fish cannery (at this time Monterey's sardine industry was in full swing). However, cannery worker or not, when word of her title got out, she became something of a local celebrity.

The house the baroness lived in was built in the early 1900s and still stands near the heart of Pacific Grove. After her death her spirit apparently stuck around, since various people claim to have seen and felt her presence as she strolled about the neighborhood. One individual who occupied the house after her death spoke of a spirit that appeared in the building. On one occasion this individual mentioned the presence and the house she lived in to her tennis partner (the man who told me this tale). Needless to say, he was flabbergasted to learn that the house had belonged to his grandmother! When he excitedly asked about the presence, the lady unknowingly described the baroness to perfection! To illustrate this point, the man said that his grandmother was in the habit of letting her hair down and wearing a white dressing gown to bed—exactly how the lady described the image she had seen. With such a coincidence almost too much to believe, the twosome made immediate plans to meet again. On this occasion the man brought with him a picture of the baroness. Upon being shown the picture, his tennis partner stated emphatically that there could be no doubt. The lady in the picture was the woman she had seen in her house!

## The chair floated near the ceiling...

*May 13, 1990* A Monterey resident of approximately seventy-five years reported a ghost in the house he and his family had lived in for twenty-five years. Among the manifestations were the sounds of footsteps when no one was there, cupboard doors that opened and closed on their own, and a kitchen faucet that turned on and off by itself. Other interesting happenings included the overwhelming odor of perfume that drifted through the master bedroom when no one in the room was wearing perfume, the mysterious turning on of the television at the same time each day, and—most amazing of all—the sight of a Lazy Boy chair floating near the ceiling!

## She saw—and heard—the Man in Gray...

*May 16, 1990* This incident took place at the Naval Postgraduate School when I was being interviewed for a brief appearance on local television. The interview was to publicize a ghost talk I was scheduled to give after the school's annual Concert in the Park. After I told a few tales, the gentleman who set up the interview wondered whether a long-time waitress at the school (who was serving lunch in the ballroom) could share a story or two about the Man in Gray (see "The Man in Gray," page 80). Upon being asked about the building's best-known ghost, the waitress (a ten-year veteran at the facility) indicated that she had heard several tales about the Man in Gray but had never experienced anything herself. Her mother and sister, however, had also worked in the dining area, and both of them had experienced ghostly happenings—mainly "feelings of presence" and "taps on the shoulder." On one memorable occasion, though, her mother (who had worked at the facility for approximately twenty years) had both seen and heard the Man in Gray playing the piano in the La Novia Room! Unfortunately, when the gentleman who set up the meeting telephoned the waitress's mother, she graciously declined to be interviewed for television.

## Upon checking into the history of the house . . .

*June 15, 1990* A lady who once lived in an old house near Monterey's Royal Presidio Chapel told me about a number of ghostly happenings that took place there. Among the weird occurrences were the sounds of music that could be heard when the oven door was opened! Other sounds of a more ghostly nature included those of footsteps and the opening and closing of upstairs doors. The footsteps were most often heard climbing a flight of stairs. When they reached the top, the sounds of a door opening and closing could be heard. Next there would be more footsteps (as if someone was crossing the upstairs landing), followed by the opening and closing of a second door. All the sounds were very distinct, and all were heard by several people over a period of many years. As would be expected, all the sounds took place when no one was around to account for them.

Upon checking into the history of the house, the lady learned that a suicide had once taken place on the property. Further research turned up one other significant fact. The room at the end of the landing had been the bedroom of the person who committed suicide!

# Postscript

With this collection of notes having come to an end, I would like to thank the many people who shared their stories with me. Without these people this book would not have been possible. Among the folks who are represented in this work are numerous old-timers from around the Monterey Bay area. It is their stories that I frequently find to be among the most fascinating. Not only have they experienced many remarkable things, but the happenings they discuss are often associated with the numerous historic structures that are found throughout the Monterey Peninsula and its surrounding communities. With tales of the strange and unexplained becoming a part of the history of these buildings, I think many people will agree that they take on an added, mystic dimension that adds a bit of spice to what might have been a somewhat inactive "afterlife."

In addition to the old-timers who shared their accounts, I wish to thank those who sought me out and told me about the haunted happenings they or their acquaintances have experienced. I realize how difficult it must have been for some of these people to share their stories with a stranger, particularly one who did not profess to be an expert on the subject, and whose primary interest in collecting the tales was to preserve a previously unrecorded part of our past (and, as it turns out, part of our present too).

Among the other people I do not want to forget are the numerous individuals who took my college classes and who enthusiastically sought out and interviewed several long-time residents of the Monterey Bay area. Found within this text are selected notes that have been adapted from these interviews. I wish to thank the students for their interest, and the individuals they tracked down for the tales they told.

Perhaps, at this time, it is appropriate to point out that these tales are only examples of the fascinating stories old-timers have to tell. I believe it is important for all of us to seek these people out and to record their accounts before they (and their stories) become ghosts themselves. After all, what is history but accounts of the past? And without *all of the accounts*, our stories remain incomplete. It is unfortunate that the most colorful parts of our past are often lost to historians, as tales of the strange and unexplained—as well as other items of local interest—are frequently omitted from history books. Of course there are several reasons for this, among them being the difficulty of documenting such happenings and the belief that they are not as important as facts and figures, or other, more "noteworthy" events of the day.

As I close the file on twenty years of ghost notes, I find myself once again confronted with a question that constantly comes up in talking with people about ghosts. Even after countless conversations with people who have experienced the unexplainable, I can't say for sure that I believe in ghosts. This is not because I discount the stories that have been shared with me; instead, it is because I have a difficult time understanding what a ghost is. Unfortunately, the word conjures up different things to different people. To some a ghost (or a ghostly tale) brings to mind a grisly account of blood and gore, while to others a ghost (or a ghostly experience) means nothing more than a fleeting glimpse of a familiar face—an image that evokes a memory (or serves as a reminder) of someone who has gone on before. In fact, as these notes show, ghostly tales include many kinds of weird happenings.

So, to date I haven't been able to come up with a direct yes or no answer to the question of whether I believe in ghosts. However, in response to (and in defense of) the many people who shared their experiences with me, I will say that I believe something is happening that I, for one, do not understand. In many of the cases recorded in this work I think something out of the ordinary did take place. There have been too many people over a period of too many years, and from too many walks of life, who have experienced events that defy explanations for me to shrug off the incidents and say that they were merely coincidences, bad dreams, figments of the imagination, or drug-induced visions. Whatever the explanations may be, it's a safe bet that *something* is happening!

Peculiar happenings continue to take place, but I find it difficult (or unfair) to blame all of the odd incidents on ghosts. However, I will say that I am continuing to collect stories of the strange and unexplained, and if a *Ghost Notes Two* ever comes out, I can guarantee the reader some fascinating accounts about some fascinating events . . .

# Index of Locations

This index lists only selected locations, omitting private homes and other sites that are not accessible to the public. In addition to the specific places listed here, readers will also note that a number of Monterey Bay area locations and communities, including several outside the Monterey Peninsula proper, are mentioned in the text. Page numbers for photographs are in **boldface**.